Out of Justice, Peace

Winning the Peace

OUT OF JUSTICE, PEACE

Joint Pastoral Letter
of the West German Bishops

WINNING THE PEACE

Joint Pastoral Letter
of the French Bishops

Edited and with an Introduction by
JAMES V. SCHALL, S.J.

Appendix: "Towards a Nuclear Morality" by
BASIL CARDINAL HUME

IGNATIUS PRESS   SAN FRANCISCO

With ecclesiastical approval
© Ignatius Press, San Francisco 1984
ISBN 0–89870–043–4
Library of Congress Catalogue Number 84–80018
Printed in the United States of America

CONTENTS

5

ACKNOWLEDGMENTS

The English translation of the German bishops' pastoral letter, *Gerechtigkeit schafft Frieden*, was prepared for the bishops by Irish Messenger Publications.

The English translation of the French bishops' pastoral letter, *Gagner la paix*, was prepared by the Reverend Michael Wrenn and was copyrighted in 1983 by the *Wanderer*.

Cardinal Hume's letter appeared in the London *Times* on November 17, 1983.

Ignatius Press gratefully acknowledges the permissions it has received to use these items in the present book.

RISK, DISSUASION AND POLITICAL PRUDENCE

THE GERMAN AND FRENCH BISHOPS'
APPROACH TO PEACE AND WAR

During 1983, three major Roman Catholic hierarchies, the German (April 18), the United States (May 3) and the French (November 8), saw fit to publish detailed statements on the relation of Christian reasoning to questions of peace and war in the nuclear era.[1] In addition, the British Primate, Basil Cardinal Hume, wrote a brief, pointed letter (November 17) on this difficult subject. As these are the major Western powers with deterrent capacities, either nuclear or conventional or both, and with large Christian bodies in their citizenry, the argument of these ecclesiastical bodies is of particular interest to everyone seriously endeavoring to understand the nature and limits of civil power in this area. For the state has the obligation to defend justice, independence and civic freedom, while preventing all war, not merely nuclear, if possible.

None of these analyses, of course, can claim to be definitive. Nor, in Catholic understanding, can any particular hierarchy or combination of hierarchies by themselves do more than present their views. They must allow dissenting opinions within their own membership and permit the views of other hierarchies to be heard and considered openly by their own people. All of this should be in subordination to and in cooperation with the Holy See. Considered public opinion from all informed sources should be expected and welcomed. Moreover, the laity, as those recognized in Catholic teachings and democratic traditions to be most directly responsible for public life and its civil defense in organized societies, have a right *not* to be bound unduly by the private views of any hierarchy when there are in fact broader views current in the Church—among Catholic political philosophers and from the Holy See. A very wide range of

---

[1] The Dutch bishops have also made a statement, as have the Irish bishops. The latter, "The Storm That Threatens: Joint Statement by the Bishops of Ireland on War and Peace in the Nuclear Age", July 1983, is available from the Catholic Press and Information Office, Dublin.

relevant opinions is open to civil and military leaders, as well as to the citizenry, in these questions. Truth and integrity require that they be free to avail themselves of these options in a reflective and responsible manner.

John Paul II, for his part, had already set forth the general principles to be observed in these considerations, particularly in his addresses of January 1, 1982, June 11, 1982, November 12, 1983, and the World Day of Peace, 1984, together with numerous others.[2] Naturally, Catholics in particular remain at liberty to follow the Holy Father in all these areas. Each of the episcopal positions deserves consideration. Each, taken separately or especially together, permits a wide degree of freedom and judgment about what is at stake and how to meet the actual problems facing free societies as they seek legitimately to defend themselves and guarantee their freedom in a realistic fashion.

Intelligence normally multiplies freedom and options. What seems characteristic initially of European statements is their refusal to allow fear and the climate of fear, so prevalent in the media and in many peace demonstrations, to decide this issue. "We resist the temptation to indulge in resignation and illusion," the German bishops add, "even if these seem very near at hand. We have firm confidence that the logic of the arms race will be overcome." (GB no. 155).[3] A wise use of intelligence, force, politics and prudence can insure that our civilization need not fall into some sort of apocalyptic despair. This itself is a climate which is or becomes a political tool capable of being used for ideological ends. That existence and civilization are beset with risks, then, is not necessarily an evil, even if this means we must live in dangerous circumstances. To assume that the *only* alternatives are total destruction *or* surrender necessarily narrows the scope in which choices less drastic in nature might legitimately be considered and taken. The German and French bishops have, therefore, widened the basis of discussion. In their documents, there is a certain welcome, courageous confidence which our society, after so much pessimistic rhetoric, needs to hear. That there is danger is not doubted. But neither is the possibility of good men and women finding acceptable alternatives doubted.

---

[2] Both the English edition of *L'Osservatore Romano* and *The Pope Speaks* will be the normal source for the many statements of John Paul II in this area. The two particular addresses mentioned here, along with many other public statements pertinent to this theme, will be found in *The Apocalyptic Premise: Nuclear Armament Debate* (Washington: Ethics and Public Policy Center, 1982), Document no. 24.

[3] References to the German bishops' letter and to the French bishops' letter will be cited as GB or FB, followed by the paragraph number in this edition.

Since the United States pastoral letter on war is generally available and widely distributed in a number of versions (the United States Catholic Conference, the Daughters of St. Paul, *The Tablet*, the *Congressional Record*, *Origins*), it seems both useful and necessary to make these remarkable European reflections easily obtainable, in one handy volume, to everyone who reads the United States document or its summaries. The issue in itself has aroused widespread interest and invites careful attention to all sources. As analyses of the topic itself and as indications of the diverging views of various local hierarchies, these French and German positions in particular serve to place the reasoning and considerations of war and peace in a much more complete theological, moral and political context.

The present volume, then, containing the German and French pastorals, with an appendix of the letter of Cardinal Hume, is presented out of an interest in and a sense of responsibility to the whole range of legitimate views present in the public order and acknowledged in the Catholic Church. But these documents are more especially gathered here because of the intrinsic worth and merits of the actual arguments elaborated by the European bishops. These documents are intended for all— clergy and laity, military and civilians, politicians and citizens, religious and nonreligious people of all persuasions—who think objectively about war and peace in a moral, religious and political context. What is important finally is the argument and its persuasiveness.

REVELATION AND POLITICS

Be it noted in the beginning, however, that Christians have a revelation to which they profess to adhere. They recognize that other men and women of good will do not follow them here (FB no. 58). But this deposit of revelation, which is considered to be open for anyone to inspect and consider in its own credentials, does not directly contain, in Christian thought, any specific formula with which to answer all difficult questions that might arise in the on-going history of human affairs. The German bishops put the matter well:

> [The Church] knows that in the present day Jesus' message of peace cannot be translated immediately into current political reality. The Church cannot declare that the words of the Sermon on the Mount constitute ethical norms for political activity which would

11

in themselves be binding without due consideration of the given circumstances and goods. . . .

The words set out in Matthew 5:39 that we should "resist not evil" are not a new and more radical law from which individuals or the state could in all circumstances derive a commandment to renounce the use of force. Where such a renunciation takes place at the expense of the well-being of others and of third parties in particular, it may even militate against the intentions of Jesus (GB nos. 42 and 45).

Revelation, then, does not substitute for politics, but seeks to make politics more itself in the circumstances in which it actually exists and operates.

It is clear, then, that revelation was not intended to make automata of men and women in responsible positions, nor was it designed to deny the validity of natural political or economic reasoning, let alone substitute a local bishop or papal decree for the appointed political authority whenever a difficult case should arise for consideration and action. Human beings must continue to use their practical reason, a reason to which certain questions deriving from revelation are legitimately directed. Similarly, reason properly poses to revelation questions arising from human experience and thereby becomes capable of receiving revelation's illuminating response. This revelation, in the Christian view, sheds light on human worth and destiny, but it does not give specific, detailed economic or political policy solutions in lieu of proper local action. Decision and action will still require experience, insight and judgment on the part of the human politician or agent.

THE GENERAL EUROPEAN APPROACH

Cardinal Hume's remarks can perhaps serve as an apt summary of the general direction of the European hierarchies:

> Inevitably . . . the peace movements bring pressure to bear primarily on the governments of the West and not on those of the East. . . . No one can deny the moral dilemma which faces us today. On the one hand, we have a grave obligation to prevent nuclear war from ever occurring. On the other hand, the state has the right and duty of legitimate self-defense. Although nothing could ever justify the use of nuclear arms as weapons of massive and indiscriminate slaughter, yet to abandon them without adequate safeguards may help to destabilize

12

the existing situation and may dramatically increase the risk of nuclear war (Hume, nos. 5 and 6).[4]

These very careful words reflect the realism which must always be present when this topic is considered. Here, the initial disadvantage of free societies is frankly recognized in the one-sided political effect of the peace movements, themselves requiring careful analyses of their own particular intellectual, ideological and financial sources.[5]

The whole issue must not be so simplified that the real problems facing political and military leaders in free societies are obscured. The obligation to prevent war is not stated by Cardinal Hume as if the corresponding and probably greater obligation of defending justice, freedom and independence did not likewise exist (GB no. 152). Massive and indiscriminate destruction in the use of nuclear arms is ruled out, but the question of tactical and controlled use is not (GB no. 92).[6] Finally, it is observed, the

[4] It is valuable to compare Cardinal Hume's position with the remarkable statement of Prime Minister Margaret Thatcher before the United Nations Disarmament Session on June 23, 1982, found also in *The Apocalyptic Premise*, Document no. 31.

The remarks of Professor E. B. F. Midgley of the University of Aberdeen are pertinent also in the light of Cardinal Hume's closing remarks: "It may well be that, if Western governments were drastically to revise their nuclear deployment and policies to bring them into accord with morality, whilst the Soviet Union maintained its present postures, the West might find itself without a sufficiently effective deterrent. The consequence of that might well be the advance of atheistic communism leading to the persecution, the imprisonment or the martyrdom of those who would remain true to the faith (The collapse of the Western powers would remove that Western pressure which indirectly limits the present intensity of Soviet persecution in various parts of their empire). . . .

"It would be unrealistic to think that the Western powers would be likely to agree to change the main Western nuclear deployment (and its associated strategies) to make it compatible with morality unless and until the Soviet government were to make simultaneous corresponding changes in its own nuclear preparations. It is not in accord with right reason for those who may feel frustrated in this situation to undertake such activities as cutting the perimeter fences and attempting to effect an entry into Greenham Common cruise missile base." (Forthcoming in the *Canadian Catholic Review*.)

Cardinal Hume, however, is careful not to oppose the ethically *required* political choice of the lesser evil to "morality".

[5] See the essays on the peace movements of V. Bukovsky (no. 12), Rael Jean Isaac (no. 11) and John Barron (no. 10) in *The Apocalyptic Premise*. See also James V. Schall, "The Intellectual Origins of the Peace Movement", in *Justice and War in the Nuclear Age*, ed. P. Lawler (Washington: University Press of America, 1983).

[6] In an extremely influential article in *Etudes*, François Gorand wrote: "The debate about nuclear weapons concerns, in the first place, Europe. It is possible that the moral considerations placed in the forefront by the United States pastoral letter ally themselves with arguments touching the credibility [of deterrence] vis-à-vis the adversary and its

very abandoning of nuclear arms might, instead of preventing their use, increase its likelihood (GB no. 104).

The Western powers not only want to prevent the nuclear might of the Soviet Union from being used on them, in this view, but also from being used on, say, China or India, both of which nations also possess nuclear arms. This larger context is, no doubt, the central one: How in fact do we prevent *all* nuclear war, given the nature of the weapons, the nature of the enemy, the nature of moral reasoning, and human nature itself? The Central Committee of the German Catholics, in an earlier document, was careful to note that we must strive to prevent *all* wars, nuclear or conventional.[7] The German hierarchy acknowledged this also (GB no. 142) and recalled that many wars have been fought since the end of World War II, with the loss of thirty to thirty-five million lives, in nonnuclear confrontations (GB no. 3).

In general, the German and French bishops paid much more attention to the nature of the ideology found in the forces opposing democratic societies (GB nos. 76–81; FB no. 8) than did the United States bishops, though the latter did not neglect this point either. Likewise, the European bishops analyzed more thoroughly the *political* context in which weapons exist and threaten rather than the physical weapons themselves, which seems to have been more the focus of the United States document.

---

acceptability by public opinion, which are the arguments of the strategists of 'no first use'.

"But from a European point of view, these considerations do not make reality disappear. The facts are that the commitment by our allies not to have recourse to nuclear weapons first would mean that we accept the perspective of a conventional defeat, since, in the European theatre, it is the threat of the nuclearization of the conflict which compensates for the conventional inferiority of NATO.

"The United States bishops, as partisans of the 'no first use', answer: Correct the conventional inferiority. Now, on the one hand, everyone knows that the Europeans do not have the means to attain such an objective, not only on the financial level but also, the United States bishops should reflect, in human terms.

"Faced by the militarized states to the East, can we come up to their level without ourselves being militarized? And on the other hand, suppose that one day we did establish conventional equilibrium in Europe; all history shows that such an equilibrium is very much less stable than a nuclear equilibrium. Put in other terms, a 'conventional deterrent' would render very much more probable a war in Europe which, for not being nuclear, would not be less mortal." François Gorand, "La dissuasion nuclèaire: Questions aux évêques américans", *Etudes* (October, 1983), 380.

[7] Central Committee of the German Catholics, *On the Current Peace Discussions* (Bonn: November 14, 1981). Text in part is reproduced in *The Apocalyptic Premise*, no. 23; the whole text is in *Catholicism in Crisis* (1983) and will be in Ignatius Press' forthcoming *Politicians, Soldiers, Clerics, Professors: Catholic Readings on Morality and Deterrence*, ed. James V. Schall.

However, one must not view specific weapons or systems in isolation from the general context of the strategy to which they relate. If the deterrent is intended to establish above all a political objective for the chosen weapons within the framework of preventing a war, then these weapons must be judged primarily in those terms (GB no. 143).

All the documents agree that war is a dangerous path, to be avoided with great energy. But the way this might be accomplished in practice receives notably different treatments in the general discussions. This is to be expected in all practical decisions.

All hierarchies, moreover, agree that our actions should be moral. They ought to protect the innocent and the weak. They ought to be effective for the legitimate purposes for which they are designed. The primary purpose ought to be to deter war, while not losing freedom or dignity. All the bishops acknowledge and accept the idea, so much stressed by John Paul II, that men are obliged to search out better ways, so that the clear dangers of deterrence can be minimized, however much the estimation of the difficulty may vary. They believe with the Holy Father and the German bishops that "this dialogue is not utopian" (GB no. 7). On the other hand, "the Church is aware of the limits of dialogue and even of its ambiguity," as the French put it (FB no. 44). In these documents, then, we find a studied and concerted effort not to oversimplify, not to overlook relevant facts or neglect dominating ideologies, which may convert dialogue into monologue, into an exchange of the mutually deaf (FB no. 43).

EXPERIENCE AND PRUDENCE

The German bishops introduced their reflections with a lengthy and detailed discussion of the biblical notion of peace and the history of the just war doctrine as it was developed in Western Christendom and which has governed Catholic thinking in this area (GB nos. 57–65; FB no. 52). The German bishops noted that, despite the frequently heard accusation that religion has done little to mitigate war, an honest analysis of the record does not bear this out if we do not demand an impossible, nonhistorical sort of solution (GB nos. 66–72). The German bishops also stressed the fact that the peace of Christ is not primarily achieved by human effort, nor is it political. "The Christian faith knows that peace in this world and in this time will always remain under threat and that the presence of God's rule can never be realized completely or in one single design. The final state of peace cannot be achieved in the shape of any new political order" (GB no. 103). And the French bishops added, in the same vein: "Final peace is only to be found with God, beyond death. It is received as a gratuitous gift. But it is prepared for during this life" (FB no. 63).

Thus, revelation does claim the possibility of addressing mankind as a whole, so that the harmony of revelation and reason furthers what men are to be about in their own legitimate, this-worldly enterprises.

> The promotion and maintenance of peace depend not only on the policies of states but also on the attitudes of individuals and social groups. None of these spheres lie outside of the principles governing a reasonable system of ethics. For this reason, the Church claims the right to make a moral judgment in regard to political matters if the basic rights of the individual or the salvation of souls demand this (GB no. 12).

What governs this discussion, then, is primarily "a reasonable system of ethics", which includes the policies of states and the attitudes of individuals and groups. Revelation pertains directly to individual dignity and the personal salvation flowing from it and offered by God. But these are to be considered in such matters insofar as they clarify "a reasonable system of ethics" as it pertains to public issues (GB nos. 155–56). The Church does not here claim, whenever important matters arise, to substitute herself for the authority of the state in its own competency. Rather, she suggests that by force of argument and spiritual insight she addresses herself to what is in fact reasonable in a particular case, something to which all men might, on reflection, agree on grounds of evidence.

In this context, it is of particular significance that the French bishops emphasized the centrality of the virtue of prudence in these difficult matters, to suggest that we will not and cannot have that theoretical certainty in political and practical matters that might be expected in speculative sciences or mathematics (FB no. 18 and note 10). The ability to provide explicit, certain answers in any practical political case of doubt is at first sight, perhaps, tempting as a pragmatic test of the supposed "worth" of religion. But if religion could provide this in the sphere of politics, it would mean the abdication of the concrete moral subject matter of politics (GB no. 90). To hold such a position would, logically, deny real political freedom and make revelation a sort of super-executive guardian in public affairs. Experience and prudence remain central to the actual political enterprise.

Perhaps, in this connection, it is well to recall the caution of C. S. Lewis, the great English writer, on this very issue:

> The whole question of the atomic bomb is a very difficult one; the Sunday after the news of the dropping of the first one came through, our minister asked us to join in prayer for forgiveness for the great crime of using it. But *if* what we have since heard is true, i.e., that the first item on the Japanese anti-invasion programme was the killing of every European in Japan, the answer did not to me seem so simple as all that. . . .[8]

If the German and French pastoral letters do nothing else but caution us against the transformation of complex political issues into simple moral ones, they will have served the true demands of peace well. The point of C. S. Lewis' remarks is, indeed, taken up in all three European documents: the problem of the greater and lesser evil in political prudence, an issue to which we shall return.

BLACKMAIL

In one sense, the most interesting word to appear in the German and French pastorals, used also by Cardinal Hume, was the word "blackmail" in the context of political strategy about nuclear weapons. Early in their document, the French bishops said, "Yet violence and oppression exist: Would not an unconditional refusal to defend oneself provide an opportunity for blackmail?" (FB no. 2). The point at issue was that political goals can sometimes be achieved, not by war, but by its threat. Where there is a lack of courage or effort or willingness to take risk, a shrewd enemy can gain its objectives by something less than war. Indeed, it would seem that this situation of blackmail is what the European bishops think more than anything is going on in this whole debate. This is why their most fundamental stress is on politics rather than on weapons. To understand what is happening, we must pay attention primarily to ideology and intention, not to physical weapons themselves (FB no. 25).

[8] C. S. Lewis, Letter to Mrs. Edward A. Allen, undated, 1951, in *Letters of C. S. Lewis*, ed. W. H. Lewis (New York: Harcourt, 1966), 225. For Lewis' more extended discussion of this point and the issues at stake, see his "Why I Am Not a Pacifist", in *The Weight of Glory* (New York: Macmillan, 1980). See also James V. Schall, "Religion, War, and Political Theory", *Catholicism in Crisis* (January, 1983) and "Civil and Military Responsibility for a Just Peace", in *Vital Speeches* (November 15, 1983).

The Augustinian flavor of the German bishops' remarks on this issue of blackmail is worth particular consideration:

> The willingness to achieve reconciliation and peace must therefore include a sober and vigilant consideration of the treacherous and perfidious nature of evil in the world—otherwise it can easily succumb to the illusions of Lucifer. We must not overlook the drastic situation and the frailty of our world which, despite its redemption, still faces great travail.
>
> For this reason, the Church has always adhered to the necessity of protecting the innocent against brutality and oppression, combating injustice and defending justice and righteousness. As we know from the lessons of history, a universal renunciation of this protection and resistance may be understood as weakness and possibly as an invitation to perpetrate political blackmail. In fact, such a renunciation may foster the very things which it is designed to prevent, namely, the oppression of the innocent and the infliction of suffering and brutality on them (GB nos. 103–104).[9]

The duty to protect the innocent, by force if necessary, by persuasion preferably, is the task of government. "This protection is, first and foremost, the task of the government, which can also avail itself of the powers of the state—within the limits imposed by the ethical code, law and constitution" (GB no. 105).[10] Within the state, this legitimacy cannot be denied (FB nos. 13 and 14). In external relations, where there is in fact no authority competent to fulfill this service, "there is no denying a state the right to an ethically permissible defense in certain circumstances" (GB no. 106). The German bishops preferred to call this a doctrine of "just defense" (GB no. 107).

---

[9] On Augustine, see the chapter on war in Herbert Deane, *Political and Social Ideas of St. Augustine* (New York: Columbia University Press, 1956); Henry Paolucci, "St. Augustine and the Uses of Force," *Fellowship of Catholic Scholars Newsletter* (December 1983).

[10] See Yves Simon, *The Philosophy of Democratic Government* (Chicago: University of Chicago Press, 1951), "The Instruments of Government", 108–27.

DISSUASION

The French word for "deterrence" is *"dissuasion"* (FB no. 28).[11] This seems, in many ways, to be a better word to express the sense of how the European bishops think we do and ought to confront the nuclear issues. If war is to be avoided, we must confront not so much weapons, but wills behind political powers. Wills can be affected by weapons, no doubt. But they must be primarily addressed by a reasoning system that makes it clear that certain paths must be avoided (GB nos. 136–151). The French bishops state the issue cautiously:

> Nuclear deterrence has not prevented some atrocious wars since 1945. One hundred and thirty conflicts which have taken between thirty and fifty million lives have been counted. But it has staved off the direct suicidal confrontation between the superpowers. It cannot be denied that deterrence has played a certain regulatory role; it serves as a fundamental but nonetheless dangerous wisdom, for if fear can be the beginning of wisdom, it is not wisdom itself (FB no. 33).

Politics and politicians gain their meaning and dignity from this context, the context of successful "dissuasion" whereby worse evils are successfully avoided by show of force or preferably reason.

Recalling that World War II largely came about because of blackmail and the refusal of the British, French and United States governments to "dissuade" the Nazi regime in time, and adding that our present situation is "not without analogy" (no. 8), the French bishops wrote:

[11] "If it does not want to find itself in such a situation, the only course open to the Western alliance by way of a response is to equip itself with comparable weapons within a collective security system. Only in that way can it defend itself against political coercion and make it clear to a potential aggressor that the attempt to translate his intentions into reality by the use of force entails considerable risks for him as well. That is essentially what the *policy of deterrence* is all about. It aims at making it clear to an adversary that the trouble and expense of launching an attack or an attempt at coercion are out of proportion to the benefit to be derived from such an action and are therefore not advisable.

"*The French term for this concept is 'dissuasion'. More effectively than the German word 'Abschreckung', or the English equivalent 'deterrence', it places the issue at stake into the proper political context.* Under the given circumstances, then, nuclear weapons are also a means of preventing war and thus of maintaining peace. Without a quid pro quo and without a reasonable chance of making peace secure in other ways, it is impossible to dispense with them." Central Committee of the German Catholics, *On the Current Peace Discussions*, 14. Italics added.

> Frankly, no one wants war—least of all the specialists, better informed about the risks at stake. . . . Some countries are very well-skilled at seizing the advantages of war without paying the price of its having been unleashed: Simply by fomenting the threat of war, they commit permanent blackmail (FB no. 7).

The German and French stress on the legitimacy of "just defense" in confrontation with a known enemy, armed in a known way, motivated by a known ideology, gains particular force in this regard.

Carefully thinking within this approach, then, the problem is to avoid capitulation *and* to avoid war. Both aspects must always be kept in mind in any policy. "The central question which is being asked, then, is the following: In the present geopolitical context, can a country which is being threatened in its life, liberty or identity morally have the right to oppose this radical threat with an effective counter-threat, even one which is nuclear?" (FB no. 20). The European bishops give a guarded, careful positive answer to this question in a climate of risk and dissuasive, deterrent force. The French bishops then acknowledge that the threat "of nuclear conflict is not illusory" (no. 5), but they also think that "the suicidal nature of such a conflict makes it improbable but not impossible" (no. 5). Politics cannot deal with impossibilities, since it deals with actions which can be otherwise, but it can deal with improbabilities. That is, it can "dissuade". It can direct a variety of arguments and forces against the wills that are likely to use blackmail or power to achieve their known, announced ends, which are to be taken seriously and, if successful, would corrupt the very possibility of civilization.

The German statement is something of a masterpiece on this point:

> The discussion about safeguarding peace and freedom is today largely confined to military strategies and arms questions. As a result, the general public gains the impression that peace policy consists above all of security policy. . . .
>
> The first principle applicable to the maintenance of peace in the narrower sense of the term—including and indeed especially in East-West relations—consists in what we have already observed in general about the requisite degree of protection against brute force and oppression, about the defense of law and justice and about relations with other states, including those of our opponents. There are chiefly two threats looming ahead. The first is the danger to the freedom of nations and their citizens from totalitarian systems which disregard elementary human rights in their sphere of dominion and which might be tempted to use their power for expansion or for the

application of political influence and extortion. The second danger lies in an escalation of armaments with an immense accumulation of nuclear and conventional weapons which, as many people fear, might one day cause the catastrophe of an outright war. *We must counter both dangers simultaneously–above all by political means* (GB nos. 129–30. Italics added.).

There is not just one fear but a double fear, both of which must be met. And it is not insignificant, in this reasoning, which threat the German bishops placed first. The primary means to meet *both* of these threats are *political*; that is, while not neglecting military strategy, which itself is mainly political, a political dissuasion that would guarantee both objectives can and must be constructed by free men.

Thus the notion that there is only one danger, massive death, and this the most important one, is not worthy of free men and women. The French bishops were particularly clear in spelling out the very dubious grounds on which much of the current anti-war rhetoric rests, when placed against more enduring and noble values of civilization:

> Does not the absolute condemnation of all war place peace-loving peoples at the mercy of those who are motivated by an ideology of domination? In order to escape war, these people risk succumbing to other forms of violence and injustice: colonization, alienation, privation of their liberty and their identity. When played out to the end, peace at any price leads a nation to every kind of capitulation. A unilateral disarmament can even provoke the aggression of one's neighbors by feeding the temptation to seize a prey which is all too ready for the taking (FB no. 9).

This practical realization which recognizes that an ostensibly noble and pure position can in fact lead to evil consequences places politics back at the center of the discussion. Politics is that discipline and action which must account for where things are most likely to go in fact, not merely in hope or in theory. The German and French bishops insist that there are many more than one dire evil which must be accounted for. Peace at any price does not lead to peace at all. The German bishops even touched on the theological reason for this realism characteristic of classical Christian thought: "He who lived a life of nonviolence became a victim of violence and thus disclosed the abyss of human violence. Since then, it has formed part of *the realism of the Christian faith* invariably to see the gospel of peace in the context of the power of sin" (GB no. 34. Italics added.). This recapitulation of Romans 13 requires that we know the difference between good intentions and good actions, between what ought to be and what is.

The European bishops argue for a steady, clear-sighted and firm political position, which directs itself to the real spiritual causes of peace, religious and civil. This does not neglect the reality of force in the world, which can be used both for good and for evil purposes. What is of primary concern is the will of an enemy who might produce and use weapons. How do they think of weapons in their own terms? Do they agree that war is totally unacceptable? Any refusal to look coldly at such issues is contrary to prudence and risks misunderstanding the real source of the problem facing actual politicians. It also renders any long-term peace in freedom impossible.

The European bishops have stoutly refused to be panicked by fear or deluded by false ideological promises. In this sense, they have served to calm an overly charged debate. They have not been inattentive to what the ideologies say of themselves, nor to the relation between theory and practice. The French bishops, after noting the former democracies in Eastern Europe now under the control of "Marxist-Leninist ideology", and not denying in the least the serious problems existing also in the soul of the West, continued:

> [The Marxist-Leninist states] sometimes even make disciples in systems which are directly opposed to them. But it would be unfair to put everyone in the same category and close our eyes to the aggressive and dominating character of the Marxist-Leninist ideology. In this ideology, everything, even the aspirations of nations for peace, must be utilized for the conquest of the world (FB no. 8).

This clear understanding that movements for peace are or can be political tools of an ideology as well emphasizes again the correctness of the European bishops' view that the primary issue must be seen to be political.

The German bishops, in a more lengthy discussion, traced this sort of ideology back to its origins, to a certain secularization of Christian concepts, to the hope of actually achieving the Kingdom of God in this world (GB no. 75). And they frankly recognized that the real causes of the present military confrontations rest principally in this ideology and its premises:

For Marxist-Leninists, world revolution remains an ideologically indispensable hope which so far has not been abandoned. Apart from a number of other factors, the East-West conflict rests primarily on this doctrine of deadly enmity between revolutionary socialism and capitalism. This doctrine cannot be simply identified with a policy of military expansion, and it therefore calls for a separate confrontation on the intellectual and political plane (GB no. 81).

Again, this means that we must look at the real causes of war and its prevention in intelligence and will, in political "dissuasion".

The European bishops, then, are not afraid to think about weapons within a strategy of risk and prudence, one which will not provoke war nor yield liberties and values constitutive of civilization itself. Again, this requires an understanding of what politics is about. In order better to understand the position of the French and German hierarchies, particularly on what they say about nuclear threats, it is well to recall a long passage in Jacques Maritain's *Man and the State* in this context:

> Politics is a branch of ethics, but a branch specifically distinct from the other branches of the same stem. For human life has two ultimate ends, the one subordinate to the other: an ultimate end *in a given order*, which is the terrestrial common good or the *bonum vitae civilis*; and an *absolute* ultimate end, which is the transcendent, eternal common good. And individual ethics takes into account the subordinate end, but *directly aims* at the absolute ultimate one; whereas political ethics takes into account the absolute ultimate end, but its *direct aim* is the subordinate ultimate end, the good of the rational nature in its temporal achievement. Hence a specific difference of perspective between those two branches of ethics.[12]

Maritain here, following Aristotle, was not saying that there is no ethics to politics: quite the opposite. He attacked pure Machiavellianism which denied any ethical element except power and its success. But this still required attention to the different situation of the politician and the individual in matters of public choice, a difference grounded in reality itself. Thus, different sorts of problems and situations will often come before a politican in his official life that will not occur in his private life.

Maritain went on:

> Many patterns of conduct of the body politic . . . such as the use by the state of coercive force (even of means of war in the case of absolute necessity against an unjust aggressor), the use of intelligence services

---

[12] Jacques Maritain, *Man and the State* (Chicago: University of Chicago Press, 1951), 62.

and methods which should never violate the human rights of people but cannot help being rough with them, a lot of selfishness and self-assertion which would be blamed in individuals, a permanent distrust and suspicion, a cleverness not necessarily mischievous but yet not candid with regard to the other states, or toleration of certain evil deeds by the law, the recognition of the principle of the lesser evil . . . all of these things are in reality ethically grounded.[13]

These distinctions and observations are perhaps subtle, even obscure, but they are vital if we are to understand how the German and French bishops argue, and argue ethically, that is, rationally and politically. "The rationality and wisdom which must be expected of the holders of political office", the German bishops wrote, "cannot be replaced by observance of our Lord's precepts" (GB no. 46). That is, by virtue of its peculiar subject matter and complexity, the holders of political office must be able rationally and wisely to see the real choices that lie before them.

The question arises particularly in the area of legitimate defense: Are there cases in fact which arise for the ethical and responsible politician or soldier in which there are, objectively, no good alternatives of action or non-action, but which require him in some way to act or not to act? The case C. S. Lewis mentioned above might be an example of this: If the ethical "choice" not to drop the bomb on the Japanese cities would have left as a question of fact only two alternatives—a massive invasion, killing many millions of Japanese civilians and soldiers together with allied soldiers, and the slaughter of the captive Europeans besides, or eventual submission to the aggressor with the same result—the choice, and not merely the toleration, of some evil would have been inevitable. If by hypothesis there are only such evil choices, what is to be done and on what principles? Would political life have to be abandoned, and if so would that choice not also be itself an evil?

The German and French bishops, along with Cardinal Hume, address this problem in principle. First of all, they agree that certain actions are evil—the indiscriminate and unnecessary bombing of civilian targets, for example. But they likewise acknowledge that surrender is also an evil and will lead to equally serious evils, perhaps greater ones, since they are not merely questions of life but of willed deformity of life. Secondly, they insist that the political nature of the issue be kept in the forefront of the discussion. That is, they understand that the threat to use nuclear retaliation, even against enemy cities (the French deterrent, FB no. 28), is itself

[13] Ibid., 62–63.

part of the possibility of effective deterrence or dissuasion. The French bishops themselves put it this way:

> It is in order not to wage war that nations seek to show themselves capable of waging it. Peace is still being served when the aggressor is discouraged and constrained to the beginning of wisdom as a result of an appropriate fear. The threat of force is not the use of force. It is the basis of deterrence [*dissuasion*], and this is often forgotten when the same moral qualification is attributed to the threat as to the use of force (FB no. 26).

Maritain's point about the specific nature of political ethics is illustrated in this consideration. There is no attempt to praise this condition, but there is an obligation to acknowledge its existence.

THE LESSER EVIL IN POLITICS

The French bishops insist that an enemy have no illusions about the threat. Obviously, if an enemy knows that it is only bluff, it is no threat. Some hold that this very willingness to use these weapons as threats—which is necessary, as the German bishops likewise acknowledge, if they are to impress anyone in the first place—is itself immoral (GB no. 141). In general, the European hierarchies do not accept this latter position because they understand the nature of political reality in the present conditions, the kind of reality the honest politician and soldier have to live in, in which there are in fact powers and wills motivated by ideology and ambition, which are in fact restrained immediately only by fear and uncertainty, consistent with their own announced ideology.

> After all, weapons only provide an effective deterrent if their use can be threatened in a credible manner. From the standpoint of preventing war, however, the main elements of the strategy of deterrence are the mutual threat of unacceptable levels of destruction and the attendant risk. Precisely the prospect that conventional or nuclear war cannot be limited poses for one's opponent an incalculable risk which is intended to guarantee the mutual deterrent against war—any war. The use of a threat of mass destruction which one must never carry out—a morally intolerable concept—is regarded as being particularly effective for the purpose of preventing war. This immense tension is only acceptable if the whole range of security policy is directed towards the goal of preventing war and if

the military measures remain integrated within the higher-ranking concept of maintaining peace by political means (GB no. 146).

This passage in particular unifies the themes of risk, deterrence and political prudence. It warns against doing what is evil, yet acts within a political reality where other evils must also be prevented.

The European bishops are not so-called "consequentialists", who suggest we "do" evil to promote good. But neither are they determinists or non-actors or thinkers who refuse to accept probable consequences as elements of practical reasoning. They do not refuse to act when in the political sphere every option looks, and all may be, evil in one sense or another. They are not willing, furthermore, to accept the imposition of the worst regime simply because an abstract theoretical argument can apparently provide no other alternative. They have, in fact, along with responsible, active politicians in their own countries, attempted to state the most reasonable and effective option for human beings who want to remain free and to avoid war.

Here is how the European bishops state the issue:

1) Faced with a choice between two evils, both of them all but unavoidable, capitulation or counter-threats, one chooses the lesser without pretending that one is choosing a moral good (FB no. 29. See also FB no. 5 on the question of something "less totally immoral".).

2) This view recognizes that, because of the world situation, deterrence may be accepted as the lesser of two evils, without in any way regarding it as good in itself. Furthermore, this view can be held even by those who reject the morality of nuclear deterrence. It constitutes an acknowledgment that even a morally flawed defense policy cannot simply be dismantled immediately and without reference to the response of potential enemies (Cardinal Hume, no. 10).[14]

3) We are choosing from among various evils the one which, as far as it is humanly possible to tell, appears the smallest (GB no. 153).

4) It would seem to be evident that a government possessing a deterrent of nuclear arms, which threatens to make use of them, finds itself in a near occasion of grave sin. One could respond that we do not have effective international institutions to maintain peace, that is to say, so long as a country cannot really give up its deterrent without grave risks for its own liberty as well as its cultural and spiritual

[14] See note 4.

26

values, that near occasion of sin is what moralists call a "necessary occasion". It is necessary to accept this occasion as a compromise so long as there cannot be created a balance of confidence and discussion which ought to replace the present balance of terror. We must remind nations of the grave obligation which they have, at the present time, of rendering remote this occasion of sin and showing themselves prepared to accept limitations on their normal sovereignty in the measure necessary to create an effective international authority (Archbishop Beck of Liverpool during Vatican II, quoted in FB, note 20).[15]

These passages each refer to the political order, to the realization that no positive good choice may in fact exist and that each choice or non-choice, in fact, directly results in some dire evil of a political or military kind.

It is in this very precisely delimited context that the European bishops ask what is the right sort of defense permissible for honest soldiers, politicians and citizens seeking to confront *all* the issues involved, not just one or two. Their answer, almost with one voice, is "Choose the lesser evil", which is the classical Thomist position. They recognize that even the judgment about which evil is "lesser" is itself a question of prudence in moral-political affairs. They suggest that the "dissuasion" system, both in its general Allied and in its particular English and French forms, is the choice of a lesser evil, the one most likely to prevent war, preserve some liberty and lead to a less dangerous situation if pursued with courage and prudent persistence in the face of the recognized and serious risks.

In this context, the German bishops ask whether "weapons designed to deter and to prevent war [may] be meaningfully used in a war pursuant to the principle of the proportionality of means" (GB no. 149). They worry about escalation. They answer their own question, however, forthrightly, "We hope and pray that a situation will never occur in which somebody is confronted with such decision-making" (GB no. 150). That is, they think that if the morally acceptable policy of deterrence is followed in a political context, the situation will not arise. But if it does, it is to be decided by the "somebody confronted with such decision-making", that is, the politician—to be decided with as much prudence as possible, keeping all goals in mind, in terms of the lesser evil.

[15] Regarding the sort of international order at issue, the German bishops remark: "Such a world authority designed to protect freedom and peace must not be created along the lines of a centralist unitary state. The principle of giving help to those who practice self-help forms the necessary adjunct to the principle of solidarity among all nations" (GB no. 128). See also Bishop Roger Heckel, S.J., *Self-Reliance* (Rome: Pontifical Commission on Justice and Peace, 1978).

The French bishops answer substantially the same sort of question in this way:

> We will not enter into the technical debates of specialists regarding the credibility of our defense, regarding the deployment of our classical, nuclear, tactical and strategic means and their relationship to and compatibility with other systems of those involved in a common alliance. Each poses specific ethical problems which call for the virtue of prudence: the morality of an effective retaliation by conventional arms, first use of tactical nuclear strike (only in principle), response by a second strike, and so forth. Other problems arise with respect to articulation of the relationship with one's allies, the control of action by political power and up to what point, and so forth. In these very technical problems, which have an ethical dimension, we must guard against two extremes:
> 1. To renounce any ethical judgment as if one were going to leave these matters, so fraught with human significance, solely to a technical logic.
> 2. Peremptory judgments of the deductive type which would make light of the complex technical problems involved.
>   Between these two extremes, it is appropriate to formulate a prudential judgment which adheres closely to the contingencies that have been weighed with great circumspection and which recognize the interplay of certitudes and questions: a respect for the nature of what is at stake and for the value of responsible statements is required here (FB nos. 17–18).

What is remarkable about this very penetrating statement is its willingness not to give a prefabricated religious answer to difficult concrete problems that will come up. It respects the politician and soldier in their own office. It tries to indicate the relevant principles, the necessity of prudential judgment of the particular case by the politician or soldier. The German and French statements agree in not locating the final moral choice outside the responsible politician who must act as best he can with all the information available but with no absolute certainty or clarity.

NONVIOLENCE AND SOLDIERING

Is nonviolence an option? Many have begun to argue that some theory of nonviolence must be substituted at the state level for such defense policy. The European bishops are careful not to affirm directly that the state is

28

itself somehow an "object" of revelation as the human person is. Secondly, they do not rule out this non-violent option for some individuals, but only under the condition that this be not itself a cause of greater evil in practice. Finally, they suggest that nonviolence is not internally or externally an option for the state. The French bishops acknowledge the usefulness of private nonviolence in some cases, but still wonder:

> Can we declare that these methods are effective to the point of rendering superfluous the necessity of an armed defense? One can well imagine what slaughters would be produced by resistance and even a passive resistance among entire peoples who are without external military supports and are handed over to less scrupulous tormentors (FB no. 15; see GB nos. 46–48).

"Can nonviolence be a policy for states?" the French bishops also ask. "The Church has always recognized the right that political powers have to respond to violence by means of force. Christ did not contest the authority of Pilate (Jn 19.11)" (FB no. 12). "The Church does not encourage exaggerated pacifism. She has never preached unilateral disarmament, knowing full well that this could be a signal for violence on the part of an aggressive military, political and ideological complex" (FB no. 35).

Just as the possibility of some individual non-violent position is allowed, provided it does not jeopardize the innocent, so the German and French bishops also consider the vocation of the soldier. They are quite frank in acknowledging the central position of the military, even in making possible the very existence of non-violent options in the light of modern ideologies which forbid them when they come to power.

> The safeguarding and promoting of peace constitute central tasks in politics. . . . A soldier who serves in order to safeguard peace must withstand the tension of knowing that he is arming himself on behalf of the state, preparing to fight and learning to do something which he hopes that he will never have to perform, because there is nothing that he desires more resolutely than to preserve peace without the use of force and to resolve conflicts by means of negotiation.
>
> Those who refuse to perform military service for reasons of conscience have also to live to an equal extent with another strain: If everyone were to follow their example, this would create a vacuum of power which can lead to vulnerability to political blackmail. . . .
>
> If and as long as security policy pursues ethically permissible and indeed obligatory goals—prevention of war, defense of ethical and

political values against totalitarian threats and the promotion of disarmament—and avails itself in this of ethically acceptable methods and means, then the service rendered by soldiers is both indispensable and morally justified (GB nos. 199–202).

CONCLUSION

The French and German bishops sought to account for the order of politics without at the same time denying the primacy of the spiritual. They recognized the temptation to present a purely spiritual answer, which would ignore the dire threats that confront free peoples. Answers utterly devoid of practicality and realism lead people to forget the ethical enterprise altogether and turn simply to Machiavellianism, as Maritain warned. Thus, men needed, on the principle of reason not being denied by revelation, a fair statement of principles, of what politics and military force could do to work for higher ends. The European bishops did not doubt that a sort of materialism was also a problem in the West as well as the East, though in divergent varieties (FB no. 59).

> A people cannot live for a long time with its eyes riveted upon the radar screens of its territorial surveillance or upon the statistical charts of its economists. All this is important but remains in the order of means. Beyond the means of living arises the question of the reasons for living: for persons, but also for nations and for the entire human race. And this is a question of culture—that is to say, a spiritual question (FB no. 55).

The whole question of politics and deterrence has its proper place only if we understand the values existing in the whole.

Thus the German bishops stress a point that John Paul II has frequently emphasized: that spiritual purposes come first for the Church and yet are essential if there is to be any possibility of changing what are in fact difficult political conditions and realities.

> Prayer contains the roots of the spiritual and moral strength of the reawakening needed by the world in order to take decisive steps towards peace. . . .
> It is not possible to achieve peace without changing standpoints and patterns of conduct which proceed on the basis of our own personality and our personal interests more than that of our neighbor and his interests and more than on the basis of the whole and the common good. An alteration of one's perspective so that we do not

look at the others from our point of view but at ourselves from their point of view possesses fundamental importance for everyone and in particular for Christians (GB nos. 171 and 177).

In short, these German and French documents remind us that "there remain questions to which various answers are possible among Christians" (GB no. 16). But there are ways to reason carefully and prudently even in the face of grave moral and military threats. Quite without prescribing concrete solutions or moralizing, we have here two reasoned, hopeful statements which serve to restate the Christian tradition in the light of the realities of our time.

OUT OF JUSTICE, PEACE

JOINT PASTORAL LETTER OF THE GERMAN BISHOPS

I. INTRODUCTION

(1) "The gospel of peace" is a biblical name for the message proclaimed by Christ. Hence, when we speak of this message, we must also speak of peace. At the same time, peace is one of those words which are pronounced by people throughout the world frequently, vehemently and with the greatest concern. The peace which Christ brings and promises is very different from the peace which the world can give or take, win or lose. But God's greater peace has a great deal in common with mankind's yearning for peace: It calls upon us to serve peace both between individuals and among nations; it lays down the criteria for this service, it points the way ahead and it inspires us with strength. The Church of Christ and the bishops are therefore summoned, in our present circumstances, to proclaim the words of the prophet, "Justice creates peace", and also to set out the conclusions which follow from these words for our conduct and our action in the world today.

1.1 The Call for Peace

(2) In view of the incredible destructive power of modern arms, the call for peace has assumed a special degree of urgency. Wide sections of our youth as well as people of all age groups are now voicing their yearning for peace. In East and West alike, the arms spiral continues to grow and prompts many people to ask in their anxiety when the threatening accumulation of destructive weapons will finally thrust mankind into the abyss. Many people can no longer understand a world in which it is possible to place missiles and weapons in the most remote corners of the globe whereas there still prevails in those same places a lack of rice, bread and medicines.

(3) Admittedly, we have been saved from the outbreak of a world war for over forty years. Following the horrors of the Second World War, the work of promoting understanding and reconciliation between hitherto alienated nations has made encouraging progress—particularly regarding the relationship between our own people and the French and Polish nations. Nevertheless, nearly one hundred and thirty wars which cost the lives of thirty to thirty-five million people were waged in the Third World during this period of time. In Europe, too, we witnessed the use of military force: in East Germany (The German Democratic Republic), Hungary, Czechoslovakia, Poland and Cyprus. Despite various negotiations and the numerous resulting agreements and treaties, the tensions and differences between the political blocs and between individual states have not diminished.

(4) The different forms of discord in our world cannot be explained by a single cause. Many factors converge in this field: differing views on universally binding ethical norms, an expansive power policy, the expansion of one's own sphere of political interest, the pursuit of economic interests, the fear of privileged groups about losing their power, a hostile view of other nations and the existence of prejudices.[1] One of the main causes underlying the East-West conflict consists in the tension between the ideological claim advanced by the communist system—based as it is on class warfare and world revolution—and that concept of human life which calls, instead, for a free legal and social order as the basis of mankind's existence.

(5) The peace of the world in this situation cannot be explained and demanded in terms of simple formulas. We often construe peace as a process directed towards a reduction in the use of force and an increase in the rule of justice. The promotion and the maintenance of peace are closely

[1] Cf. the resolution adopted by the Joint Synod, "Der Beitrag der katholischen Kirche in der Bundesrepublik Deutschland für Entwicklung und Frieden" (The contribution by the Catholic Church in the Federal Republic of Germany for development and peace; cited hereafter as EF and the section number) 2.1.2, in *Gemeinsame Synode der Bistümer in der Bundesrepublik Deutschland: Beschlüsse der Vollversammlung*, official complete collection, 5th ed. (Basel, Freiburg, Vienna: 1982), 492.

The papal and conciliar pronouncements are first cited, where possible, in reference to the official editions and the authentic original texts. A large part of these texts as well as the statements on peace by the Catholic Church in the Federal Republic of Germany can easily be consulted in *Dienst am Frieden: Stellungnahmen der Päpste, des Zweiten Vatikanischen Konzils und der Bischofssynode, 1963–1982*, 2nd rev. ed., Verlautbarungen des Apostolischen Stuhls no. 23, cited hereafter as VAS 23 and the page number; and in *Frieden und Sicherheit*, Arbeitshilfen 21. These documents are published by the Secretariat of the German Bishops' Conference and may be obtained direct from them at Kaiserstrasse 163, D–5300 Bonn.

interlinked in this context. Our task is to preserve and to develop our own system of life. We must endeavor to establish a wider measure of social justice in the world. We must endeavor to find sound ways of banning hostilities and the use of force.

(6) The debate about the right way of achieving these goals leads in itself to friction and dispute. The true answer to anxiety and impatience is the spirit of strength which clearly discerns, accepts and survives the impact of reality. The true answer to escapism or a blind aggressiveness is the spirit of prudence, which does not fear the toil of taking one small step at a time. The true answer to egoism and fanaticism is the spirit of love, which esteems the dignity and the liberty and the rights of each individual and which protects our neighbors against degradation, bondage and injustice. Unless everyone declares his willingness to conduct a dialogue, the work of peace and the policy of peace cannot be carried out.

1.2 The Necessity of Conducting a Dialogue

(7) In his World Day of Peace message on January 1, 1983, Pope John Paul II issued an urgent appeal to mankind: "The means *par excellence* is to adopt an attitude of dialogue, that is, of patiently introducing the mechanisms and phases of dialogue wherever peace is threatened or already compromised, in families, in society, between countries or between blocs of countries."[2] This dialogue is not utopian. It is founded on the very nature of man: "Every person, whether a believer or not, while remaining prudent and clear-sighted concerning the possible hardening of his brother's heart, can and must preserve enough confidence in man—in his capacity for being reasonable, in his sense of what is good, of justice, of fairness, in his possibility of brotherly love and hope—to aim for recourse to dialogue and the possible resumption of dialogue."

(8) The Pope also refers to the attitudes necessary to ensure the success of a dialogue. These consist above all in mutual frankness and acceptance. A dialogue presupposes that each side will accept the different nature and the special features of the other side: "We must not renounce, through cowardice or constraint, what we know to be true and just, for that would result in a shaky compromise."

(9) In this letter, we bishops take up the call proclaimed by the Pope and

---

[2] "Der Dialog für den Frieden: Eine Forderung an unserer Zeit", no. 2 in *Dokumentation 5/1982* (press service of the German Bishops' Conference, December 12, 1982). Pope John Paul II again broached one of the three main objectives named by Pope Paul VI in his first encyclical *Ecclesiam suam*.

invite everyone concerned for peace to conduct a dialogue. To begin with, we appeal to our congregations and associations. In view of the wide range of the discussions and the expectations placed on the Church, we also extend a wider invitation to the general public, including in particular the decision-makers in society and state, training and education, and the mass media.

(10) We are well aware that many people base their arguments for peace on the Bible. Above all in the Sermon on the Mount, Jesus provides occasion to those who have nothing to do with the Church to formulate proofs and arguments which sometimes contradict each other. It seems to us imperative to voice a few words of explanation. What is the meaning of "peace" as used in the Bible? What consequences follow from the biblical concept of peace for contemporary problems? Nor can the vicissitudes of historical developments be disregarded. The questions and answers of today lie more deeply rooted in the past than might appear at first sight. Precisely the experiences of history teach us the close connection between the understanding and the practical possibilities of peace and the underlying concept of man. Emphasis should be placed upon this reciprocal relationship so as to permit a better assessment and judgment. Above all, we shall not evade the concrete questions inherent in the promotion and maintenance of peace—questions which today afflict so many people. Finally, we wish to give an impetus within the Church in particular but also within society in general towards the enhancement of our work towards peace. Although we remain aware of the limits to our competence with regard to practical political measures, we cannot evade our responsibility in the sector of ethical principles.

1.3 The Tasks Facing the Church

(11) The mandate of the Church is to furnish testimony of the gospel to mankind. The Church proclaims to the world the reconciliation with God bestowed upon us through Jesus Christ and the concomitant hope of peace. The mission of the Church "does not relate to the political, economic or social sector, since the goal which Christ set for her belongs to the religious sphere. Nevertheless, there flows from this religious mission the mandate, the light and the strength needed to help the human community to build up and strengthen the world in accordance with divine law" (GS 42).[3]

---

[3] The Pastoral Constitution of the Second Vatican Council on the Church in the Modern World, *Gaudium et Spes*, cited hereafter as GS and the section number.

(12) The promotion and maintenance of peace depend not only on the policies of states but also on the attitude of individuals and social groups. None of these spheres lie outside of the principles governing a reasonable system of ethics. For this reason, the Church claims the right to make a moral judgment in regard to political matters if the basic rights of the individual or the salvation of souls demand this (GS 76).

(13) The Church has to fulfill her own intrinsic task in promoting peace throughout the world. She must teach the gospel to all people. Because of her universality, she can form a very close link between the various human communities and nations (GS 42). The Church makes no distinctions concerning outsiders and foreigners. Her mission places her in close proximity to everyone. Those who belong to the Church are linked with the whole of humanity, and they are obliged to share mankind's hopes and joys, cares and worries. This imparts to the Church a unique strength in joining together individuals and nations.

(14) The Church feels a particular sense of mission in the work of promoting peace on behalf of law and justice, development and progress, and a fair distribution of the earth's goods. She regards "this concern . . . for the future of man on earth and therefore also for the course of the whole of development and progress as an essential, unbreakably united element of her mission" (*Redemptor Hominis*, 15).[4] The Church will undertake a direct role herself in this concern by means of her own works and services.

(15) The Church's contribution towards the maintenance of peace is of a different nature. One of the foremost duties of a government's policies lies in protecting the legal order at home as well as the existence and freedom of a nation against aggression and extortion from outside. This imposes an onerous political responsibility on the bearers of governmental authority, and they have to discharge this duty with their own skill and competence. In this, Christians will be guided by the gospel and thus also by a fundamental Christian understanding of man and the world.

(16) As far as a military contribution towards peace-keeping is concerned, this field of competence incumbent upon the state does not fall outside the ethical principles of responsible political action. Today, a keen discussion is in progress about the goals of military peace-keeping as well as the choice of means adopted to this end. We bishops feel called upon to express our views on this: We would not only like to recall the applicable moral principles, but also to name the criteria which permit the appli-

[4] Pope John Paul II, encyclical *Redemptor Hominis* 1979, cf. *AAS* 71 (1979): 257–324 = VAS 23, 194–208.

cation of these principles to concrete questions. Nevertheless, there remain questions to which various answers are possible among Christians, too. Let us therefore bear in mind the exhortation of the Second Vatican Council:

> Very often their Christian vision will suggest a certain solution in some given situation. Yet it happens rather frequently, and legitimately so, that some of the faithful, with no less sincerity, will see the problem quite differently. Now if one or another of the proposed solutions is too easily associated with the message of the gospel, they ought to remember that in those cases no one is permitted to identify the authority of the Church exclusively with his own opinion. Let them, then, try to guide each other by sincere dialogue in a spirit of mutual charity and with anxious interest above all in the common good (GS 43).

2. THE BIBLICAL CONCEPT OF PEACE

2.1 Fundamental Perspectives

(17) The Christian understanding of peace is rooted in the biblical testimony to the promise of peace by God. This promise of peace by God inspired the history of his people under the Old and the New Covenant alike. This promise was given to a world marked by conflict and war. In our faith, we know that God has already begun to fulfill his promise through Jesus Christ. Through him, peace is granted to us as a gift of God. But for us Christians, too, peace remains a gift which we do not yet have at our disposal but whose perfect manifestation we still look forward to—a gift for which we pray.

(18) Revelation testifies to an understanding of peace which cannot be confined to political peace. It is more deeply rooted and wider ranging. When Paul the Apostle speaks of "the peace of God, which is greater than all understanding" (Phil 4:7), he is speaking of that peace which links individuals and peoples together under given social conditions. This peace possesses its own conditions which we cannot prescribe. Nevertheless, according to God's will these conditions ought to impinge upon the current existence of mankind in such a way as to permit the fulfillment of peace—as it were, as the anticipation of that peace which only God can grant us.

(19) The biblical testimony presents us with fundamental principles. When the Holy Scriptures in the Old and New Testaments speak of peace, they do not limit it to the resolution of disputes between nations or the settlement of hostilities and wars among states. On the contrary, they testify to the history of God's relations with mankind and they show in the light of that testimony by what means God's desire for peace among humankind and through human beings can be realized.

(20) The biblical understanding of peace is shaped by its understanding of man: of his vocation to enter into communion with God and with the community of men and women which thereby becomes possible. It is determined by man's sinful rejection of God and thus also of his fellow men. It is determined too by his redemption which bestowed upon us access to our Father, thus opening the way towards a new relationship between people. For the Bible, these points of view are quite inseparable: Only where God reveals himself to man and where he is recognized and glorified as God, and thus only where man can live in peace with God, can a comprehensible, durable peace also exist in human relations. Peace with God, peace with oneself, peace in one's own heart and peace among mankind all belong together.[5] The will to peace and man's capacity for preserving peace must be judged in the light of our salvation if we are not to succumb to a faulty assessment of the possibilities of peace. Such a realistic and simultaneously hopeful view of man will enable us, even in the face of today's challenges, to find paths which do not end in resignation because of resistance encountered in the world but which lead us towards our true goal, because God comes towards us to meet us on the way.

(21) This tension between eschatological endowment and present-day tasks is typical of the biblical understanding of peace. It offers not only a vision of final peace but also encourages man to realize here and now as far as possible the order of peace ordained by God and to do so within the earthly limits of human existence.

---

[5] Under the influence of the concept of peace developed by St. Augustine, for whom true peace can only exist in connection with justice, writers have referred since the twelfth century to a threefold peace. For example, Berthold von Regensburg (1260) stated in his 17th sermon "On Peace": "The three kinds of peace are the following: The first peace is peace with God. . . . The second peace . . . is peace with oneself. The third peace is peace with your neighbor." In *Die Missionspredigten des Franziskaners Berthold von Regensburg*, ed. Franz Gobel, preface by Alban Stolz, 2nd ed. (Regensburg, 1857), 260 f.

2.2 "Peace—the Work of Justice" (Isaiah 32:17)

(22) Amidst the glad tidings proclaimed in the Old Testament stands the God of Israel, who is not only the God of a single nation but also the Creator of the world who wishes that all men be saved. Israel became the people chosen by God, distinguished by the Covenant and ordained to become "a witness to the people" (Is 55:4). God led this nation along its various paths and provided its law so that it could find life (cf. Dt 30:19).

(23) However, the Old Testament testifies not only to the promise of a life of justice and peace, which Israel is intended to obtain in union with God; it also contains numerous descriptions of acts of violence and wars which Israel carried out against other nations and in which it became entangled. The history of God's chosen people is, in many cases, not an ideal history of peace. Despite this, however, peace within the nation and between states retained its claim and its urgency for Israel. It meant more than simply the absence of war.

(24) Israel saw a life conducted in peace as an expression of God's salvation. People wish each other "Shalom", i.e., peace, as the manifestation of life lived in freedom, justice and security. People saw peace as being guaranteed by their covenant with God. Even a merely temporary peace among men is for them the result of God's work and salvation for his people. Peace exists not only in a truce and in the security which Israel attempted to acquire by means of agreements and treaties, but above all in concordance with God and with the order of life bestowed by him. Peace represents well-being for the whole nation and its individual members founded on God's covenant. The disloyalty of the nation towards its Lord God constitutes a danger to peace. The biblical concept of peace thus possesses a religious as well as a socio-political dimension which are closely linked together in the history of Israel, but which tended to be separated from one another in times of weakness (exile, apocalyptic).

(25) Israel preserved peace by realizing peace within the nation in response to God's gift of the Covenant. Peace found concrete expression in the justice given to every individual in his relations with his neighbor. This justice, which God explicitly demanded in his commandments, was not an onerous duty which limited the freedom of man: It was intended to stamp the life of the individual and of the whole nation in freedom. Peace arose from the dispensing of justice. Indeed, peace gained its first sound foundations when God proclaimed justice within the nation and made it the yardstick for the behavior of everyone towards his neighbor. For this

reason, the prophet Isaiah proclaimed peace as "the work of justice" (Is 32:17). This meant that peace was realized within the communal existence of man, not by itself because of its natural virtue, but from the strength of God and pursuant to the criterion of his laws. Wherever man accepts God in his life, there opens up the possibility of his union with his fellow man in justice and peace. This is the fulfillment of the words of the psalm: "Mercy and truth have met together; justice and peace have kissed each other" (Ps 85.10).

(26) The peace which Israel gained through her covenant with God was also intended to prove its strength in the external relations with other nations. How did Israel react in the external crises of her society? She did not avoid the temptation of founding her security more on political alliances with the world powers than on the help of God. In his fervent words of warning, "If you do not stand by me, you will not stand at all" (Is 7:9), the prophet Isaiah reminded us of God's steadfast pledge which deserved greater trust than any diplomatic skill and military strength. God's help was not deemed to constitute a replacement for requisite military precautions. However, these finally became fatal for God's chosen people, who expected more from larger numbers of chariots and horsemen than from the "Holy One of Israel" upon whom they should cast their eyes (Is 31:1).

(27) Israel was expected to be a "witness for the nations" and to impart to them the peace which God prepares for his people (cf. Is 52:7). However, the prophets only see this universal peace mission for Israel as a future vision. "It shall come to pass in the last days that all nations shall share in it" (Is 2:2). God would then voice the law in fulfillment of his promise. The time would then come when they would "beat their swords into ploughshares and their spears into sickles" (Is 2:4; cf. Micah 4:3). This prophetic vision of peace referred to the future age of perfection. But it did not become "unreal" for Israel or even for the present believers in the words of the Lord. Rather, this vision contained a claim based on a truth that is still valid today. Wherever God's rule is recognized and acknowledged and wherever God's truth and justice prevail in the thoughts, aspirations, and actions of men, then peace in this world is possible.

(28) But Israel often gambled with God's gift of peace. The history of the Old Covenant contains many testimonies to the disloyalty, ingratitude and sinfulness of the nation and its individual members. Time and time again they worshipped all of the false gods or some of them at least. Time and time again they called for peace, but in reality it was only a

hollow and surreptitiously obtained peace (cf. Is 6:14, 8:11). Time and time again the people turned aside from the God of the Covenant and of peace and went their own wilful ways. It was at this behavior that the message of the prophet was directed. Wherever Israel rejected God's offer of peace, the promise would not be forfeited. Admittedly, this became the word of the judge and the call for a new departure. Despite the disloyalty of the people of Israel, the message was maintained, and it became the promise of a "new covenant" which contrasted with the present disloyalty towards the Covenant with God (cf. Is 31:31–34, 54:10).

(29) It is particularly the prophetic texts in the Old Testament which show how the biblical concept of peace developed. The prospect of an eschatological peace after man's earthly life does not bring about a loss of the elementary concept of peace as constituting our well-being. On the contrary, peace among individuals and among nations is placed upon a stricter footing of binding norms.

(30) Thus, in this prophetic vision, it is not the concrete historical conditions in which Israel lived, and it is certainly not the behavior of Israel herself, which was the basis for the trust that the peace of God can be realized. This makes a turning towards God, "who alone creates peace", all the more urgent (Is 26:12; cf. Ps 147:14). The relationships between people must change and the attitude of the individual must change so as to pave the way for the approaching "king of peace" and his "kingdom of peace". Hope rests on God and on his Messiah, of whom Israel expects the establishment of this kingdom of peace (cf. Zech 9:9 f.).

2.3 "He Is Our Peace" (Ephesians 2:14)

(31) The Scriptures in the New Testament show how people have experienced in Jesus "the kindness and love of God our savior" (Titus 3:4). Jesus himself is God's messenger of peace whose efforts in word and deed bring God's liberating kingdom nearer and permit the emergence of new relationships among people. The arrival of the Messiah Jesus and the acknowledgment of God's dominion proclaimed by him provide a fresh start for "peace on earth" (Lk 2:14). Jesus also takes care of people in their concrete situations in life: He overcomes their distress, he promises them forgiveness of their sins, he grants them spiritual and physical salvation and he teaches them to pass on to their brothers the reconciliation which they have gained (cf. Mt 5:25, 18:23). But in the eyes of Jesus, peace is something which is not easy to gain. The gospel which he proclaims is like a sword; it does not protect against disputes with those who oppose it.

Indeed, the gospel is thrust at them and calls with the utmost fervor for imitation. The words of Jesus, "I come not to bring peace, but a sword" (Mt 10:34; cf. Lk 12:51) do not contradict his peace mission, but demand a resolute acceptance of the gospel which imparts God's peace to mankind.

(32) Jesus' mission achieved its final and true fulfillment on the Cross. As the king of peace (Mt 21:5), Jesus arrived at Jerusalem a few days before his death. In Jerusalem, he depicted the kingdom of peace as the definitive reconciliation between God and mankind—to be achieved, not with the means of political power, but in the sign of the Cross. The price of his unique state of peace was the sacrifice of his life. When we testify to the gospel of peace, we testify to the gospel of our crucified Lord. When we accept the Resurrection of Jesus as an article of faith, we testify to our crucified Lord. Jesus on the Cross and Jesus the resurrected Savior: These are our peace. The Cross and Resurrection made up the sum total of his life and formed the basis of the peace which the world cannot give.

(33) And thus we have "peace with God through our Lord Jesus Christ" (Rom 5:1). This peace granted by God exercises a conciliatory influence among humankind if people open up their hearts to Jesus and to his movement for reconciliation. The peace which Jesus Christ established in the world of human self-righteousness, distrust and discord led to a new experience of the "forbearance of God" (Rom 3:25), fraternal trust and an understanding cooperation. Jesus Christ himself may be called "our peace" in the light of prophetic promises (Micah 5:4; Is 9:5) because he "has made both one [Jews and heathens] and has broken down the wall of partition between us" (Eph 2:14).

(34) The secret of iniquity (2 Th 2:7) and the destructive power of evil manifest themselves in full in the sight of our crucified Lord. Discord and injustice prevail so powerfully in our world that Jesus had to die in order to bring about peace and justice. In the Cross of Jesus, the abyss of human discord is revealed along with the fidelity of the life-giving God. He who had to die because of our sins revealed in his death the power of sin. He who lived a life of nonviolence became a victim of violence and thus disclosed the abyss of human violence. Since then, it has formed part of the realism of the Christian faith invariably to see the gospel of peace in the context of the power of sin.

(35) The Resurrection of our crucified Lord shows that we are sinners (cf. Rom 1–8): In our disbelief of God's promises, we ourselves try to be gods and thus cause discord and trouble. When we say that the resurrected Christ alone is our peace, we are at the same time testifying that we are without any peace when we are separated from him. We then aspire to our

safety by bypassing him and, in the final analysis, all our godless aspiration to safety only creates more uncertainty and discord—a chain of violence which never seems to end. But the more we adhere to Jesus, who finally created peace on the Cross and brought about true reconciliation, the more we can actively hope to obtain his peace for everyone without minimizing the power of our sinfulness.

(36) The Church of Jesus Christ faces a challenge to continue to testify to the peaceful words of her Lord and, in a spirit of hope against hope, to make them her own cause. In the imitation of Jesus Christ, the "ministry of reconciliation" (2 Cor 5:18) has become the most urgent task of the Church and, moreover, her outstanding characteristic. God, "who has reconciled the world to himself in Christ" (2 Cor 5:19), wishes to continue his work of reconciliation through the service of the Church. The Church accomplishes this ministry both internally and externally: She does so internally when we, the faithful, become the community of reconciliation in practice and of brotherly cooperation; she does so externally by inviting all people to found the peace of the world on a new relationship with God and in a spirit of trust in the divine order of the Lord's commandments.

2.4 "Unless Your Righteousness is Greater . . ." (Matthew 5:20)

(37) The peace which God creates permits the faithful, as messengers of peace, to become peacemakers. The faithful who work as peacemakers are fulfilling God's peaceful works. Hence, the promise made by Jesus that they "shall be called the children of God" (Mt 5:9) is meant for the peacemakers. Their endeavors on behalf of peace bring them into a special proximity with God because they testify in their deeds that God already began in Jesus Christ to create peace.

(38) The work of the peacemakers urges us time and time again to act in imitation of Christ. The Sermon on the Mount points the way forward when it places the words of Jesus among the guiding principles of a new "overflowing" righteousness intended to shape the whole life of Christians. Jesus calls for a righteousness which "shall exceed the righteousness of the scribes and Pharisees" (Mt 5:20). We must not evade this call only because we believe that it will overexert our limited human resources. Jesus himself realized this righteousness in his endeavors on behalf of mankind right up to the end of his life, and he promised those who accepted his words that they would not remain without the strength and the encouraging support of his spirit.

(39) From this trust in God's goodness acting through Jesus Christ,

there arises for the faithful a fresh capacity to do right and to fashion conditions of peace in truth and justice. Peace is therefore not only realized among the followers of Jesus in the asserting and delimiting of rights peculiar to the individual or a group, but in the learning and practicing of what is right in the face of the Lord and what is likely to promote reconciliation between men and more fraternal trust.

(40) This spirit of fraternal love is intended to help the faithful to treat the evil-doer with patience and a symbolic nonviolence: He is expected to turn the other cheek to him and to let him have his own cloak (Mt 5:39 f.). He is also expected to try to overcome the enmity of the other in the same spirit and not to exclude him from his love. When God has overcome enmity, the faithful are also called upon to overcome enmity and to create peace by reconciliation. In this way, Christians translate into practice the commandment to love one's enemy (Mt 5:43–45). In this way, they are inspired by the words of Jesus not to be afraid, to leave fear behind them and only to look for the kingdom of God and for his righteousness (Mt 6:25–34).

(41) The faithful are called upon to become peacemakers in their given relationships in life with their fellow men: "Repay to no man evil for evil. . . . If it be possible, as much as it depends on you, live peaceably with all men" (Rom 12:17). The responsibility of Christians for peace also relates to politics. Christians are expected to contribute towards creating peaceful conditions in society and also between peoples and between states. They are questioned in this as to their specifically Christian contribution to the promotion and maintenance of peace. In the first place, this contribution does not consist in a certain type of political conduct, but in the testimony for the peace which Christ gives—for the peace of God which is now spreading in a conciliatory manner among mankind.

(42) The promise and precepts imparted to us by Jesus in the Sermon on the Mount extend not only to his individual disciples but also to the Church as a whole. In her imitation of Christ, the Church as a whole is summoned to continue the promulgation of his message of peace, to testify to its content in terms of the challenges of the present age and to translate it into reality in undiminished form. At the same time, she knows that in the present day Jesus' message of peace cannot be translated immediately into current political reality. The Church cannot declare that the words of the Sermon on the Mount constitute ethical norms for political activity which would in themselves be binding without due consideration of the given circumstances and goods. Nevertheless, the Church must see to it that the words of Jesus retain their binding force for

Christian action and their challenging trenchancy in the face of all behavior based on merely human calculation, and that they are shown to be valid in any age. The Church must show that the Sermon on the Mount and its message are not directing men's attention to unrealistic, ideal conditions in some distant future but are beginning to operate here and now, even though the dimensions of the promise far exceed anything experienced so far.

(43) The demands voiced in the Sermon on the Mount do not tolerate any reductions at the expense of Christ's intentions. But what did Jesus really want? This question becomes more acute when we desire to apply his instructions not only to the ethical behavior of the individual but also to that of social groups and indeed of entire peoples and states. The imperative contained in the words of Jesus holds true for Christians at the various levels of social life—down to the political consequences. Conclusions must also be drawn for politics from the spirit of the Sermon on the Mount, which consists in the spirit of fraternal love. But how does this take place and what conclusions should be drawn? The question is about how the demands of Jesus in the Sermon on the Mount can be transferred to the social and political plane.

(44) In the Sermon on the Mount, the evangelists hand down the words of Jesus to the Christian community. The Sermon touches upon fundamental attitudes for shaping the life of Christians—fundamental attitudes which also apply to the political attitudes of Christians. However, the words of the Sermon on the Mount are not laws to be applied in systematic fashion. The antitheses in the Sermon on the Mount are intended to overcome a form of thinking and acting designed to withdraw us from our own responsibility towards God and towards our fellow men by invoking a written statute.

(45) The words set out in Matthew 5:39 that we should "resist not evil" are not a new and more radical law from which individuals or the state could in all circumstances derive a commandment to renounce the use of force. Where such a renunciation takes place at the expense of the wellbeing of others and of third parties in particular, it may even militate against the intentions of Jesus: In his name, Christians must practice fraternal love and, in the name of charity, effectively counteract the oppressors on behalf of the poor, those in need of protection and those dispossessed of their rights.

(46) It would therefore be a misunderstanding if we tried to shape and organize our social and political life directly pursuant to the words of the Sermon on the Mount. The rationality and wisdom which must be

expected of the holders of political office cannot be replaced by observance of our Lord's precepts. But such persons ought to be inspired by them. This also manifests itself in dealings with legitimate power. Particularly inasmuch as the state resists injustice and oppression by respecting human rights and protecting the innocent, it proves that it "is the minister of God" (Rom 13:4).

(47) Christian conduct which is oriented towards the Sermon on the Mount is not blind to evil. An injustice remains an injustice; the guilty remain guilty; what is lawful remains lawful. But politics should be transcended by Christians in the direction of the "righteousness which exceeds the righteousness of the scribes and Pharisees" (Mt 5:20). What is required is a creative love which remains free of hate and the quest for revenge even when combating injustice and which above all endeavors to overcome evil by attacking its roots. This love will attempt with all its force, time and time again, to win over one's opponent for peace, to find non-violent solutions to conflicts and to offer ways of cooperation. This is the way in which we should overcome the vicious circle of force and reduce aggressiveness and confrontation.

(48) Such a willingness to attempt a fresh start was founded by Jesus in his call upon us to love our enemies (Mt 5:43–48; Lk 6:27–28, 32–36). In the final analysis, this love of one's enemies is founded in God's gracious deeds, which, moreover, do not exclude those who are evil and unjust, and in God's mercy which we have experienced through the love of Jesus and which has made friends and God's children out of sinners and enemies. Loving one's enemies is and remains the criterion, the characteristic and the possibility of those who live in expectation of God's coming rule and who are inspired by God's dominion as an event which already determines the present. Loving one's enemy also wishes to teach us to understand others, i.e., our adversaries, as human beings for whom Christ laid down his life. This gives us a better understanding of their situation and their way of regarding us. Loving one's enemy makes it possible for us to resist the temptation to allow our enemies to force us to become aggressive. It opens up for us the freedom to approach our adversary without giving up the freedom to take the first step. Nor is this love discouraged by the fact that we can by no means be certain of making a friend of our enemy.

(49) We Christians must translate and incorporate this potential for Christian peace into political action on behalf of peace so that the demands of Jesus in respect of nonviolence and loving one's enemy will thereby achieve validity in social and political structures. In the nuclear age in

which the future of all of us is at stake, this orientation towards the precepts set out in the Sermon on the Mount will—as the Joint Synod noted—"facilitate our task because the message of the Bible and the needs of the present age point in the same direction more clearly than in former times" (EF 2.2.1).

(50) Irrespective of any setbacks and diversions, the demands made by Jesus in his Sermon on the Mount retain their obligatory nature for Christians, just as the concomitant promises remain in force. The important thing with regard to their realization is that the spirit of the Sermon can unfold its strength in human beings—a strength which pervades the existing realities and inspires the deeds of Christian men and women. The forms of relationships between human beings will soon begin to change as a result of the patient efforts of Christians seeking to imitate Jesus Christ—as a herald of the promised fulfillment with which God wishes to endow us.

3. PEACE AND WAR
IN THE CHANGING COURSE OF HISTORY
AND IN THE TEACHING OF THE CHURCH

(51) If we reflect on the teachings of the Bible about peace, we are confronted by the question as to the nature of the precepts issued by Jesus Christ and the apostles in the history of Christianity. Many people pose the question: Has the Church accepted the New Testament's message of peace, or has she in fact failed historically in regard to this message? Has she ever been a peacemaker on any large scale? Has she prevented wars and their consequences with her doctrine of the "just war", or has she contributed to the justification of wars in some way? Within the framework of the possibilities presented in this paper, we shall take a look at these and similar questions and attempt to answer them. At the same time, we can only mention a few chosen examples of the course taken by the Church in history—although these will be the focal points of her development.

3.1 Early Christian Testimony

(52) The early Christians had first to find their true place in the society of the Roman Empire. Their place was marked by refusal—going as far as martyrdom—as well as loyalty. On the other hand, Christians were

convinced that peace and internal security in a world dominated by the forces of evil could only be preserved by the government which "bears not the sword in vain" (Rom 13:4). For that reason, Christians prayed for all people including their rulers (cf. 1 Tim 2:1 f.). "Oh Lord, give them health and peace, concord and constancy, so that they will administer in blameless fashion the dominion which they have received from you"— that is taken from the liturgical prayer of the Roman congregation at the turn of the first century.[6] Nor could the threat of death induce them to hate their persecutors, e.g. the martyr Justin (d. circa 165); on the contrary, they wanted to convert their enemies and to lead them to eternal salvation. On the other hand, Christians remained aloof from politics. Externally, they could not be distinguished from their heathen fellow citizens; they lived with them in the same towns and houses. Nevertheless, they saw their true home as being in heaven. Because of the close links between all public institutions and the cult of the emperor and the gods, they were excluded from any active role in social life and from the acceptance of public office. A manifestation or a refusal of loyalty can be found close together in the early Christian sources, depending on whether the state authorities were convinced of the harmlessness of the Christians or whether the community was to be warned about the danger of impurity inherent in the worship of false gods.

(53) What applies in general to the attitude of early Christians to the state in general holds especially true of warfare and military service. It was not only because of Christ's message about loving our enemies and practicing nonviolence but also in their capacity as a persecuted religious minority rejected by the state that the Christians took a negative attitude towards the martial aspects of the Empire. But there were Christian soldiers, either because they had been converted to the faith during their military service or else because they had chosen this profession by virtue of their origin and family. This explains the observation by the ecclesiastical writer Tertullian,[7] who was extremely sceptical about the things of this world, that "when the Lord disarmed Peter, he was unbuckling the sword from every soldier". But even Tertullian had to admit that Christians performed their war service together with the others and

---

[6] For this section, cf. the following sources: Clemens, 1 Rom 61:1 (Fischer 102 f.); Justin, Apologia I, 57:1 (Goodspeed 67); Letter to Diognetus, 5:2 f. (Marrou 62); Tertullian, De idolatria 19 (CCL 2, 1120) and Apologeticum 30:4, cf. 42:3 (Becker 166 f. and 194 f.) as well as 38:3 (Becker 180 f.); Hippolytus of Rome, Traditio Apostolica 16 (Botte 72 f.).

[7] Cf. Apologeticum 38:3 (Becker 180 f.): "No subject is more strange to us than the subject which pertains to everyone: the state."

naturally asked God "to give all emperors a long life, and a secure empire, a safe house and brave armies".

(54) At about the same time, the Church organization under Hippolytus (d. circa 235) attempted to settle this question as follows: A Christian would not volunteer for military service, but a soldier desirous of becoming a Christian could retain his profession provided that he refrained from any heathen acts and rituals connected with this service and provided that he refused the order to kill people. This second condition was abandoned in the course of the third century. There is no overlooking the existence of Christian soldiers, including those among the combat troops and holding the rank of officers. Nonetheless, the martyrdom suffered by soldiers[8] reveals the spiritual conflict in which Christian soldiers found themselves. The willingness to perform service for the emperor reached its limits when it came to the sacrifices for the gods and the emperor: This was testified to in the martyrdom of Julius (circa 302). In individual cases, soldiers also refused to do military service—as in the case of Maximilianus (circa 295) who was prepared to accept the death penalty.

(55) In the long term, this conflicting attitude could not be maintained. Nor could the criticism voiced by the heathens be denied: The Christians benefited from the peace guaranteed by the state but did not want to help in bearing the corresponding burdens. Admittedly, Origen replied to this charge that Christians could help a state more by keeping their hands clean and praying for the just cause, the just king and for victory, for Christians could defeat by prayer the demons who instigated wars and destroyed peace.[9] Nevertheless, the number of Christian soldiers increased towards the end of the third century. In order to inculcate into them a spirit of Christian responsibility, they were referred to the sermon delivered by John the Baptist. In reply to the question put by the soldiers about what they should do, he replied: "Do violence to no man, neither accuse any falsely; and be content with your wages" (Lk 3:14).[10] One of the first heathens to be converted was the centurion Cornelius (cf. Acts 10:2 ff., 44 ff.). From then on, it was no longer ruled out for Christians to be soldiers at the same time.

(56) This gradually incipient reorientation became necessary when the

---

[8] Cf. *Ausgewählte Märtyrerakten*, revision of the Knopf edition by G. Kruger, 4th ed. (Tübingen, 1965); *Sammlung ausgewählter kirchen- und dogmengeshichtlicher Quellenschriften*, vol. 3, "Maximilian", no. 19 (86 f.): "Julius", no. 27 (105 f.)

[9] Cf. Origen, *Contra Celsum* VIII, 58, 68 and 73 (Borret 298 f., 330 f., and 349).

[10] Cf. the repercussions up to the *Decretum Magistri Gratiani*, II pars, causa XXIII, qu. 1 (Ae. Friedberg 893).

wall which divided the Church from the world and made two separate societies of them finally fell. Christians had to abandon the undivided loyalty in which they had hitherto lived as a result of their own decision and external pressure and to assume political responsibility. The exceptional situation which they had once been able to afford as a small minority was no longer possible for them. They now began themselves to share the responsibility for what they had previously accorded to the emperor from a position of critical aloofness, namely, the right to wage just and controlled wars. A testimony of this hesitant transition is to be found in the Synod of Arles (314).[11] The Synod laid down that a soldier must never quit his service but that killing in a war was not included among his duties. This again revealed the tension: It was correct to maintain the order of the state, but the great misgivings about killing in war were not simply thrust aside.

3.2 The Development of the Doctrine of a "Just War"

(57) The basic situation described above remained valid in the teachings of Saint Augustine (d. 430), who was the first to set out a wide-ranging vision of the Christian doctrine of peace.[12] He made a clear distinction between peace on earth and peace in heaven. To begin with, war was deemed a work of the devil as an expression of a state of mind which denied God and indulged in arrogance and greed. There was no doubt about the sinfulness of war. In a number of observations and in his wish to impart spiritual guidance, Augustine also approached the question— hitherto treated with the greatest caution by Christians and often adduced as a fundamental objection by heathens—as to whether there could be "just wars". Augustine added a number of concepts of ancient ethics, above all from Aristotle and Cicero, to his overall Christian approach. A war was only "just" 1) if it served the cause of peace, 2) if it was directed against an injustice (which one's adversary was not prepared to terminate or to rectify), 3) if the legitimate authorities ordered the waging of war and 4) if the war did not infringe upon the law of God. The decisive factor was the spirit in which war was undertaken by the rulers and waged by the soldiers, and also the correctness of their intentions. For Saint Augustine, it was a permanent riddle and a fatal necessity in the then existing historical situation of Christian salvation that a just cause required the use of any

[11] Cf. the problematical Canon 3 of the Synod of Arles (*Conciles Gaulois du IVe siècle*, ed. J. Gaudemet [Paris, 1977], 48).

[12] Cf. *De civitate Dei* XIX (CCL 48, 657–99).

force at all in such circumstances. The sting of scepticism about whether there can and must be such a thing as a "just" war had penetrated very deeply: "He who regards with sorrow these great, horrible and disastrous evils must admit that they are a great misery".

(58) But Saint Augustine not only turned his gaze to wars when he spoke of the yearning felt by all people for peace. He also knew of the latent discontent which prevailed at all levels of communal life: the constant danger to friendship and love in one's own home, the meanness of human jurisdiction and the difficulties experienced by all peoples in communicating with each other solely because of the alien way in which men and women encounter one another. In this life, there can be no such thing as an undisturbed and perfect system; that can only exist in the blessedness which God alone can bestow upon us. For that reason, Saint Augustine did not disdain peace on earth, even though in his opinion it only deserved the name of "consolation in misery". The system of peace based on law and justice consisted in the fact that man should "first of all not harm anyone, but also benefit his neighbor if he could". This system of life must exercise an effect, from the domestic community in marriage and family to the municipal and the state authorities to international relations.

(59) Saint Augustine thought that, at that time in world history, a perfect peace could only begin to become effective in faith and hope. He knew of the obvious opportunity for confusing peace on earth with eternal peace. For that reason, he wanted to designate the ultimate goal either as peace in eternal life or as eternal life in peace, so as to make it more comprehensive for everyone. After all, peace was such a great asset that one could not hear anything more lovely in the sphere of earthly and transient things, nor wish for anything more desirable, nor find anything better. However, talk about peace could become seductive for that very reason.

(60) Proceeding on the foundations of Augustine's philosophy, Thomas Aquinas (d. 1274) developed further the concept of a just war.[13] "Three things are necessary for a just war: firstly, the authority of the ruler (*princeps*) at whose command the war must be waged. . . . Secondly, there must be a just cause (*causa justa*). . . . Thirdly, the belligerents must have the right intention (*intentio recta*)". Only such rulers are entitled to wage war as are no longer able to turn to a judge of appeal to clear up the controversial issue. Hence, wars can only be waged by "sovereign"

---

[13] Cf. *Summa Theologica* II–II, qu. 40, art. 1–4 (Marietti 222–26).

rulers; they must ultimately preserve or search for their justice from among their own resources of power, since nobody will relieve them of responsibility for the common good of their state. At the same time, a "just war" is not justified as retribution or revenge for the injustices suffered, but in terms of restoring order and punishing a guilty party. The decision to wage war and to take hostile action must never lack the relationship with the moral order, as one cannot otherwise speak of responsible action.

(61) These observations on a just war are completely incorporated within the doctrine of moral action. The subject is dealt with by Thomas Aquinas in his comprehensive chapter on the virtue of love. War as such appears, to begin with, as a vice which runs counter to the love entrusted to man and bestowed upon him by God. War is only permissible in order to establish a peace, which in turn restores the order disturbed by a grave injustice or protects us against a grave injustice. Only a war which serves this aim is taken into consideration. If war is waged with due consideration for the common good in order to punish the guilty party, then it cannot be regarded in objective terms as a sin. A war undertaken in such circumstances is therefore not repudiated.

(62) The principles enunciated by Thomas Aquinas were adopted by all the Scholastics of the later periods; however, their application to the realities of a given situation did not engender any major changes. Since Augustine, it had been accepted that there were just wars which God himself ordained. An injustice against God such as the disbelief of heathens could thus become a just cause for war. For that reason, the permanent state of war against the heathen nations was regarded as "normal" in the Middle Ages. Thomas Aquinas was more hesitant in this field. Although the calumniation of Christ's name and the persecution of the Christians by heathens constituted reasons for war, he rejected the view that one might wage war against heathens because they did not wish to accept the Christian faith ("the faith is a matter of free will").

(63) The Spanish theologians of the sixteenth century (for example, Vitoria, Suarez, Molina) developed this doctrine further. As far as their relationship with heathen nations was concerned, they did not feel that a lack of faith and vice among heathens justified the waging of war. Nevertheless, they recognized that the violent hindrance of missionary work and the need to protect innocent persons (for example, by preventing barbaric human sacrifices) constituted a *casus belli*. Above all, they questioned the hitherto valid precondition that every just war was directed against those who are clearly guilty and who then had to be

punished as lawbreakers. At a time when nation states were emerging in Europe—states which claimed full sovereignty and did not accept any higher authority—it was pointed out that a war could be just from the standpoint of both sides. In such a case, however, the victor would be substantially circumscribed in his treatment of a defeated opponent. In this way, the conviction that just wars were possible on both sides exercised an impact upon the humanization of war. The Spanish theologians also called for appropriate mildness in the case of colonial wars.

(64) The doctrine of a just war became an important legacy of the Scholastic theologians handed down to the modern European experts on international law. But this doctrine was also subject to fundamental changes. The previously prevailing criterion that a "just war" served to punish the guilty—an increasingly difficult concept—was gradually deprived of its legitimation. The onus shifted more and more from the righteousness of the controversial issue to the legitimation of those waging the war. The sometimes generous approach which was adopted in the elaboration of reasons for waging a war (war titles) gradually blurred the distinction between generally binding legal grounds and political interests. The question as to the substantive justification for a war and thus also as to injustice and guilt in the objective and ethical sense of the expressions was banished more and more from the assessment of warfare. The doctrine of the "just war" thus became the standard pragmatic rule governing the permissibility of wars. The core of classical theological doctrine, the condition of a "just cause", had been abandoned, while the concept of a "just war" acquired a new meaning.

(65) As regards the doctrine of a just war within the theological tradition of the following period—and especially that of the Neo-Scholastics—it is a regrettable fact that it was neither brought up to date nor expanded. Moreover, these teachings moved further away from the changing political and military realities such as modern state sovereignty, the separation of politics and morals, nationalism and civil war. As a result, it was very easy to use the amended doctrine of the just war as an instrument suitable for justifying ideologies and interests which lay at a great distance from the standpoint of the Church. Today, the very different concepts of the just war are represented in many parts of the world without this leading to any major curtailment of Christian theology.

3.3 The Contribution of the Church to a Reduction in Violence And to the Maintenance of Peace

(66) From the beginning, the Church fought against abuses which derived from violence and injustice. A number of individual Christians and groups were exemplary in their fulfillment of Christ's testimony that we must love our enemies and practice nonviolence: Others proved to be peacemakers in the midst of violent confrontation. Outstanding examples are to be found in the good works of Pope Leo the Great, the Franciscan movement, the Indian apostle Las Casas, the Brothers of the Common Life, the "friend of God", Nikolaus von Fluc's Christian humanism, and the reconciliation work under Pax Christi between the French and the Germans after the Second World War (Bishop Théas). Charles de Foucauld and Maximilian Kolbe must also be mentioned in this context. However, the Church has never derived an indiscriminate rule applicable to everyone from Christ's testimony to nonviolence—as many groups tried to do in the history of Christianity and still try to do today. On the contrary, the Church has tried to open up ways of reducing the use of force irrespective of the testimony of individuals and over and beyond her continuous education towards peace. An outstanding example of this may be found in the early Middle Ages.

(67) To begin with, mention may be made of the peace aspirations of small communities which reduced the destructive impact of hostilities and exercised an integrative influence in various ways, such as the brotherhood of prayer practised in medieval monasteries, joint prayer sessions and the institution of knighthood.

(68) But unique importance was assumed after the first millennium by the "peace of God". In a society whose internal organization and legal constitution were imperfectly developed, this substantially limited never-ending private wars and incalculable brutalities. Certain persons (for example, women, children, priests, merchants, peasants) and certain objects (for example, churches, cemeteries, private dwellings, agricultural implements) were placed under the protection of God's peace in order to protect them against acts of violence and feuds. Furthermore, the use of weapons and any use of force were prohibited for certain days and times. This so-called "Treuga Dei" (literally, the truce of God) applied in general to the period from Wednesday evening to Monday morning, to Advent, the days of fasting, Easter and the more important Church feast days,

which were recognized as times of peace. During the period thereafter, many synods and ecumenical councils prohibited any use of force within the above-mentioned places and times on pain of punishment and created a formal jurisdiction of peace.[14]

(69) The issue was not simply to humanize warfare. The ultimate goal was to eliminate the use of force and to introduce peaceful ways of settling disputes. Many historians rank these efforts to preserve peace among the most successful chapters in the history of international law. They speak of great "peace movements" encompassing the whole people which, admittedly, emanated from simultaneous religious reawakening. From the twelfth century the gradually strengthening state assumed the task of maintaining internal peace.

(70) In this way, an internal sphere of peace which today seems quite self-evident to us was created through the peace of God and the law of national peace influenced by it. The right of the legitimate use of force no longer lay with various groups who conducted a feud against each other or who protected themselves by means of violent self-help. They were replaced by national legal procedures designed to bring about a peaceful and fair settlement of hostilities. The exercise of a "just power" now lay exclusively in the hands of the state. Finally, reference may be made to the peace-keeping activities of the emperor and the pope, who were able in their own way, by virtue of their honorary high status or their spiritual authority, to take action against the disturbers of the established order and to settle disputes. However, they were often unsuccessful in this. As individual states and rules had the right to maintain the peace or wage war, these efforts were often confined to mere offers of arbitration.

(71) The above-mentioned procedures for arbitration in disputes as the most important institutions for preventing war remained limited in terms of time and region. From the beginning of the fourteenth century, there arose the idea of developing into a general system the methods and procedures which had been tried out in numerous individual disputes. There arose the first great visions of a European order of peace and an international system of arbitral jurisdiction. They also contained the beginnings of what was known later under changed conditions in modern international law as a system of collective security. Indeed, international law has tried in its own way to realize many bold plans and many utopian systems that initially seemed awkward and naive—plans and systems

---

[14] Cf. Lateran Council I (1123), canon 15 (COD 3rd ed., 193); Lateran Council II (1139), canon 12 (COD 199 f.); Lateran Council III (1179), canon 21 (COD 222); cf. ibid., numerous references to individual church synodal resolutions.

which, to be sure, related in the first place to Christian Europe. The concept of the League of Nations and the statutes of the United Nations represent moves towards such a supernational organization for the preservation of a comprehensive peace order. Much of this is today still in the form of a plan—for example, the creation of a world authority for the settlement of disputes.

(72) Hence, a stock-taking of ecclesiastical peace efforts by no means proves as negative as is sometimes assumed. However, we must also recognize their limits and objectively accept them. These limits relate not only to the Church and her possibilities but also to the world as it then existed. Whereas considerable progress was made in the containment of the internal use of force by the end of the Middle Ages and the beginning of the modern period, it did not prove possible to banish wars from the sphere of international relations. The reduction in the use of force was mainly confined to the Christian spheres. For example, the crusades for the liberation of the Holy Land were sometimes conducted with great cruelty: The later non-European military encounters, including above all the colonial wars, were frequently barbaric in nature, despite many a protest by the Church. The integrative influence of Christianity itself was smashed by the emergence of religious denominations in the sixteenth century. This schism produced a new type of war, a civil war between the different creeds which entailed a particularly ruthless unleashing of force and the trend to annihilate one's adversary. This all went to show how Christians themselves can succumb, time and time again, to the temptations of power and violence and thus disregard the word of the Lord.

3.4 Changes in the Modern Concept of Peace and War

(73) We have already spoken about the modern change in the expression "a just war". This has also been accompanied by a change in the concept of peace. Without needing to set out this development in detail, it is nevertheless interesting to indicate the following basic pattern within the framework of our overall objectives.

3.4.1 The Loss of an Ethical Assessment of War

(74) In the earlier stage of modern times, war was virtually left to the discretion of those who had the authority to wage war, irrespective of whether it was a just cause or not. Relations between states rested less on

the supreme norm of justice than on rational considerations of usefulness. As a result, the classical concept of peace based on the pillars of order, law and righteousness gradually disappeared. The words of the prophet Isaiah that "the work of justice shall be peace" (Is 32:17) lost their historic impact. Up to the eighteenth century, war was clearly seen as an evil, even though it might be unavoidable and in individual cases perhaps a necessary evil. The unity between an ethical and a legal assessment of war began to disintegrate more and more. Whereas war had hitherto held its place as a makeshift device on the periphery of law for extreme cases, it now acquired a limited, albeit central, status as a legitimate means of self-help at the disposal of every sovereign state.

3.4.2 "Eternal Peace" as a Historically Realizable Program

(75) The Christian faith has always stressed that perfect peace can only be attained when the world has been perfected and history ended. For that reason, Christians have always appeared sceptical about programmatic promises of "eternal peace". Since the beginning of the eighteenth century, however, there have appeared plans designed to rearrange the Christian expectations of the future kingdom of God and to make of them a realizable scheme for a durable peace within the framework of world history. To begin with, this manifested a profound yearning for peace and a protest against a blood-stained past. In the first place, the issue was not one of future utopias. It was thought that, even if civilization remained a critical process, it would continue to advance and attain a condition of world peace founded on rationality and morality, common economic interest ("the mercantile spirit") and the fraternal unity of mankind. The conditions had to be created for this: overcoming intellectual and religious prejudices and social tutelage, discovering a harmony between economic interests and eliminating grievances in social life. Eternal peace became— and this was something new—a historically achievable program, which could be brought about under the guidance of the concept of rationality as an inherent necessity of nature.

3.4.3 The Ideologization of Peace and War

(76) Those who were certain about the advent of a realm of world peace and who saw themselves as the executive body for accomplishing it could no longer regard those who did not share this conviction as adversaries in the conventional sense of the term. They were bound to regard them as

absolute enemies who had to be destroyed in the name of future peace. Warfare between states became a war of ideas whose very nature did not permit the conclusion of a peace treaty in the traditional sense of the word. Under such a concept, wars were accepted as transitional periods and interim states of development.

(77) Wherever such expectations of a final state of peace begin to prevail, there also arise completely opposite trends. In the nineteenth century, the spread of pacifism was matched by a glorification of war. Many thinkers believed that a long period of peace engendered cowardice and effeminacy. War appeared as a prime force in human affairs, the execution of the last judgment and a means of rejuvenation of the world. Many ideologies in the nineteenth and twentieth centuries have thrived on such thoughts, which served to justify large and small wars alike.

3.4.4 War and Peace in Marxism-Leninism

(78) A major turning point came with the concept of a war motivated by the need for social revolution. It had many roots and, above all, it grew in multifarious forms as a reaction to economic exploitation. The uprising of the oppressed against their oppressors became the only legitimate application of force in history. Marxism radicalized this application of force into class warfare. The private ownership of the means of production was deemed to constitute the ultimate reason for all hostilities. For that reason, the social structures had to be radically changed by dint of any method, including that of the use of force.

(79) After Lenin, those who recognized class warfare could not help recognizing civil wars. The latter take class warfare a stage further in a natural and—in certain circumstances—inevitable manner, and they also intensify it. Class warfare becomes the central content of a just war. Hence, a war is just for the purposes of Marxism-Leninism when it benefits the advance of the revolutionary process. This applies in particular where the "bourgeoisie" has to be eliminated and "socialism" introduced. The abolition of class domination will lead to the disappearance of all wars. The collapse of capitalism after the end of class warfare will be followed by the inception of world peace.

(80) This ideology became a force in history after World War II. However, the conditions of the nuclear age rendered it necessary to adapt this doctrine. The apocalyptic conflict between revolutionary socialism and capitalism predicted by Lenin and later by Stalin no longer appeared unavoidable. The next development was the strategy of peaceful co-

existence, although enmity between the systems themselves remained insuperable. There was no peaceful coexistence in the ideological field.

(81) For Marxist-Leninists, world revolution remains an ideologically indispensable hope which so far has not been abandoned. Apart from a number of other facts, the East-West conflict rests primarily on this doctrine of deadly enmity between revolutionary socialism and capitalism. This doctrine cannot be simply identified with a policy of military expansion, and it therefore calls for a separate confrontation on the intellectual and political plane. To this must be added other factors which, in the general view, serve to determine the Soviet foreign policy and to generate tension: for example, the quest for domination, the Russian tradition of a fearful distrust, the lessons of history, the shortfall in the process of modernization, the machinery of power and the anxiety about the stability of one's own system among those nations who have been subjugated.

3.5 The Ecclesiastical Ethics of Peace in the Twentieth Century

(82) In modern times, the Church has put forward her own theory of peace and war. She defended this doctrine against the multifarious ups and downs in the interpretation of peace and war, while scarcely tackling any of the new approaches. This was destined to change at the latest by the twentieth century.

(83) The two World Wars cannot be comprehended in terms of the previous concept of military encounters, which were always seen as limited and limitable. Under these forms of warfare, the issue is no longer one of limited targets; the threat involves the annihilation of entire peoples and states. The development of nuclear weapons of unimaginable destructive power in more recent times has finally rendered it impossible to assign any positive meaning to international war in our former perception of this phenomenon. Such destructive power indicates that peace has become an indispensable condition for the survival of mankind. At the same time, the awareness of such an elementary danger has prompted louder calls for disarmament—and in most recent times, these have particularly assumed the form of radical postulates that all weapons should be abolished.

(84) The nuclear age has inspired the breaking of new ground in our thoughts about peace and war, and the full extent of this new approach cannot yet be properly assessed.

3.5.1 Modifications in the Doctrine of the "Just War"

(85) In the course of the last few decades, the teachings of the Church have faced up to these challenges more and more. Pope Benedict XV[15] spoke in 1915 of a terrible bloodbath which had been dishonoring Europe for a year and of the stupidity of this ineffably horrible war; in 1917 he spoke of the doom of "suicide". In 1939, Pope Pius XII[16] called war monstrous, and in 1943 he spoke of "walking along the edge of a precipice of unspeakable disaster" and of "destruction and carnage".

(86) Above all, Pius XII incorporated and developed the theory of the just war in its theological and ecclesiastical manifestation in the teaching program of the Church. This theory formed a focal point in his ethics of peace. War must remain a subject of ethical assessment. At the present time, it is outdated as a means for resolving international issues. The Pope called for the proscription under international law of a war of aggression and for a supranational peace organization. The "just cause" for a war focuses on a case of defense of fundamental legal rights insofar as they are directly attacked by the use of force. Hence, the previous doctrine underwent considerable curtailment and change. In view of the impact in more modern times of the secular theories of the "just war" with its many problematic forms of manifestation, it would be better and more logical to speak of a "just defense".

(87) However, Pius XII rejected any weakness which accepted peace at any price as well as a rearmament which was strong enough and desirous of depriving others of their rights. Demands were repeatedly voiced about the need for educating people in peace and training people in a Christian attitude to peace. Special importance attaches in this context to the Christmas messages of the years 1944, 1948, 1956 and 1957. Beginning in 1953, the Pope took a more detailed look at the problems of warfare with atomic, biological and chemical weapons (ABC warfare).[17] He dealt not only with the military use of these weapons but also with their political implications.

---

[15] Cf. *Die katholische Sozialdoktrin in ihrer geschichtlichen Entfaltung: Eine Sammlung päpstlicher Dokumente vom 15. Jahrhundert bis in die Gegenwart*, eds. A. Utz and B. Galen (Aachen, 1976), vol. 4, XXIX, 10 (3095); 18 (3107); 23 (3107).

[16] Cf. *Aufbau und Entfaltung des gesellschaftlichen Lebens: Soziale Summe Pius XII*, eds. A.-F. Utz and J. E. Groner, 3 vols. (Freiburg in Switzerland, 1954–1961), no. 3657 (1875 f.), 3726 (1915), 3931 (2024). Cited hereafter as UG with the marginal number, and the page number in parentheses.

[17] Cf. for example UG 2367 f. (1178) and 3849 f. (1981 f.)

(88) At the end of the 1950s, there were public debates and protests, above all in the Federal Republic of Germany, about the moral admissibility of producing, storing and possibly using atomic weapons in a defensive war. As a result of these discussions, the traditional dogma of the just war was called into question over and beyond previous objections. The political dimension of the threat from atomic weapons tended to be given less consideration in Catholic discussion in Germany, unlike the line taken in pontifical teachings as well as in discussions within the Protestant churches.

(89) The Encyclical *Pacem in Terris* issued by Pope John XXIII in 1963 showed that the new situation surrounding weapon technology was becoming a subject of ecclesiastical ethics of peace.[18] There were no debates on the permissible or impermissible use of any kinds of weapons. Time and time again, reference was made to ways of excluding war as far as possible as a means of waging politics. The Pope deplored the incessant arms race and called for an end to such competition, a prohibition of nuclear weapons and a settlement of disputes by treaties and negotiations. In our age, it was contrary to rationality still to regard war as a suitable means of restoring infringed rights (PT 127, GS 80). Pope John XXIII proposed, in an even more decisive manner than Pius XII, a world authority for the regulation of conflicts. The main attention would be directed towards promoting human rights and establishing humane conditions of life. This would also serve to bring about a reduction in the use of force.

3.5.2 The Development of the Church's Ethics of Peace

(90) In the fifth chapter of the second main part of the Pastoral Constitution *Gaudium et Spes*, the Second Vatican Council dealt with questions pertaining to peace and the community of nations (Art. 77–90). War is regarded as a set of circumstances which must be completely abolished (cf. GS 82). However, one could not deny a government the right of an ethically permissible defense if all the possibilities of a peaceful settlement had been exhausted (GS 79). In this respect, the conciliar text follows from the ecclesiastical doctrine of the just war without ever actually mentioning this expression. In the final analysis, the remaining scope for decision between surrender or self-defense will be left to the consciences of statesmen to decide; and indeed, their high degree of accountability towards

---

[18] Cf. *AAS* 55 (1963): 257–304 = VAS 23, 15–38. *Pacem in Terris* is cited hereafter as PT with the section number.

God and the whole of mankind is stressed time and time again. *Pacem in Terris* is quoted literally with reference to total war and the new weapons: "All these factors force us to undertake a completely fresh reappraisal of war" (GS 80). Total war is condemned in pursuance of papal pronouncements since Pius XII: "Every act of war directed to the indiscriminate destruction of whole cities or vast areas with their inhabitants is a crime against God and man which merits firm and unequivocal condemnation" (GS 80). The council did not state any views on the question of whether the effects of certain atomic weapons are controllable or not.

(91) The direction taken by the conciliar ethics of peace is explicit: The aim remains an all-embracing peace and the outlawing of all war under international law. The Council also provides a new orientation regarding nonviolence:

> In the same spirit we cannot but express our admiration for all who forgo the use of violence to vindicate their rights and resort to those other means of defense which are available to weaker parties, provided it can be done without harm to the rights and duties of others and of the community (GS 78).

Similarly, the Council calls upon governments to promulgate humane laws for those who refuse to perform military service for reasons of conscience (GS 79).[19]

(92) The Council does not condemn the possession of nuclear weapons; it leaves open the question of an ethical judgment of a deterrent based on nuclear weapons. The decisive pronouncement is:

> Many people look upon this [the deterrent of potential enemies with nuclear weapons] as the most effective way known at the present time for maintaining some sort of peace among nations. Whatever one may think of this form of deterrent, people are convinced that the arms race, which quite a few countries have entered, is no infallible way of maintaining real peace and that the resulting so-called balance of power is no sure and genuine path to achieving it (GS 81).

This took into account the given political realities inasmuch as such weapons can be temporarily tolerated provided that we "profit by the respite we now enjoy, thanks to divine favor, [using it] to take stock of our responsibilities and find ways of resolving controversies in a manner

---

[19] Cf. also the pronouncements of the Bishops' Synod in Rome in 1971, cf. *AAS* 63 (1971): 923–82 = VAS 23, 110–21: ". . . and all states should recognize and regulate refusal to render military service for reasons of conscience."

worthy of human beings" (GS 81). This involves less a determined stance than an emergency set of ethics on the path leading away from war and back to peace. Furthermore, the Council reaffirmed all demands made by the popes regarding the establishment of a world authority and a reduction in the causes of war, for example injustices (cf. GS 82).

(93) Pope Paul VI[20] made a passionate appeal for an end to the arms race and a complete elimination of weapons of mass destruction. Pope John Paul II[21] continued the appeals of his predecessor and founded his demands for peace above all on law and human dignity. The pronouncements became sharper and sharper against the arms buildup which brings death and destruction in its train, which leads to an outbreak of fear and which directs economic resources into the wrong channels. The present Pope made a speech before the UN General Assembly on October 2, 1979,[22] and a speech before the statue of peace in Hiroshima on February 25, 1981,[23] and he delivered a message to the Second Session of the UN General Assembly devoted to disarmament on June 14, 1982,[24] in which he warned in highly memorable words of the hour of absolute danger and the necessity of radical rethinking.

3.5.3 The Continuity of the More Modern Church Teachings

(94) The path taken by the Church's teachings on peace and war during the last thirty years reflects the changes which have occurred during this period. The statements were fundamentally different in nature, but they nevertheless had to take into account the given historical situation— thus emphasizing their developmental character and also permitting differences of regional approach. Although the doctrine of a just defense has not been abandoned, it can no longer serve as a basis for an overall concept of the Church's ethics of peace. The positive precepts on peace and the combating of the causes of war have achieved great prominence. In 1967, Pope Paul VI introduced a World Day of Peace to be observed on January 1 of each year.[25] The Synod of Bishops in Rome exhorted the world in 1974 to promote a strategy of nonviolence.[26] The resolution

[20] Cf. *AAS* 56 (1964): 55–62 = VAS 23, 39–183.
[21] Cf. *AAS* 71 (1979): 57–66 = VAS 23, 186–302.
[22] Cf. *AAS* 71 (1979): 1144–60 = VAS 23, 217–32.
[23] Cf. *L'Osservatore Romano* German ed. 10 (March 6, 1981) = VAS 23, 275–80.
[24] Cf. *L'Osservatore Romano* German ed. (July 30, 1982).
[25] Cf. *AAS* 59 (1967): 1097–1102 = VAS 23, 83–88.
[26] See note 19.

adopted at the Joint Synod on "the contribution by the Catholic Church in the Federal Republic of Germany towards development and peace" underscored the need to promote peace. Similar to other bishops' conferences, the German bishops have invariably come forward with pronouncements along these lines.[27]

(95) But it would be wrong to contrast the more recent trend in the ethics of peace since John XXIII with the doctrine on "just defense". These two perspectives supplement each other, and we cannot forego either of them. On the one hand, politicians cannot cast aside responsibility for the protection of fundamental legal rights within their political system. Where the provision of defense measures is necessary, they must take the necessary steps. On the other hand, such a "defensive" maintenance of peace is not enough. A policy of promoting peace must proceed from the assumption that peaceful relations between nations will be based less on weapons and the mechanisms of threats and more and more on respect for everybody's rights and recognition of human well-being in freedom and justice.

(96) A stock-taking of the work carried out by the Church for peace may strike many people at first sight as being disappointing. Could not the Church have assisted in the promotion of peace in a more vigorous and effective manner? We must admit that the history of the Church contains many examples of involvement in highly worldly quarrels and of a share in violence and warfare. On the other hand, what would have become of history in general and that of the European nations in particular without the positive influence of the Christian faith? We have sketched out in brief how much both international law as well as the peace-promoting and peace-keeping contribution of national law in general owe to ecclesiastical initiatives. Many movements and institutions have taken up these initia-

[27] *Gegen Gewalttat und Terror in der Welt* (1973), Hirtenschreiben der deutschen Bischöfe no. 1; *Gerechtigkeit und Frieden*, declaration of the Spring 1981 Joint Synod of the German Bishops' Conference, Arbeitshilfen no. 21, note 1; *Das Friedensproblem im Licht des christlichen Glaubens*, introductory lecture by Cardinal Höffner to the Fall 1981 Joint Synod of the German Bishops' Conference, Der Vorsitzende der deutschen Bischofskonferenz no. 8; "Frieden, wie ihn die Welt nicht geben kann: Frieden, wie ihn die Welt braucht", address by Cardinal Höffner on the occasion of the peace proclamation at the Katholikentag 1982, in *Die christliche Friedensbotschaft*, Arbeitshilfen no. 28; *Für den Frieden*, declaration of the presidents of the German Bishops' Conference and the French Bishops' Conference, Stimmen der Weltkirche no. 15.

Moreover, mention should be made of the joint pastoral letter by the Catholic bishops in the German Democratic Republic on the World Day of Peace 1983, KNA-Dokumentation no. 1 (Jan. 4, 1983); and "The Challenge of Peace: God's Promise and Our Response", the pastoral letter of the United States Conference of Catholic Bishops on war and peace.

tives in order to mitigate the consequences of armed struggles, to reduce the level of force, to make peace and to foster peace.

(97) The Christian message of peace demands that trust and a spirit of reconciliation among mankind should be realized in history by encouraging a greater willingness to conduct a dialogue. However, the peace of Christ in its complete form transcends the limits of historical feasibility. In this case, the question posed at the beginning is reversed. It is not the gospel of peace which turns out to be an illusion because of the continuous outbreak of brutality and wars. It is not the gospel which is refuted. On the contrary, the events justify the greatest scepticism about those doctrines of salvation which accept a development of mankind towards a condition of perfect humanity and peacefulness or which desire to bring about the future of an intact world by the use of revolutionary force.

4. A COMPREHENSIVE MANDATE FOR PEACE

(98) Peace is the fruit of justice. Wherever people allow God to prevail in their lives, there exist those "conditions of law" which regulate the communal existence of men and women in peace. The Christian mandate for peace demands of us that we should use all our strength throughout the world for the cause of peace (promotion of peace) just as we must try to maintain peace, however frail this may be (maintenance of peace). The gospel inculcates hope into us that our acts of peace will not be in vain (hopes for peace). The basis of this mandate for peace is its testified concept of mankind which we now wish to set out in summarized form and from which we wish to derive some fundamental conclusions.

4.1 The Ethos of Peace and the Christian Understanding of Man

(99) As we know from history, the behavior of man has been marked from the beginning by an elementary tension and by ambiguity. Man could use fire not only for warming and cooking but also for burning and ravaging; he could prepare food with stones and cut with them, but he could also wound and kill his fellow humans. Being human has always meant the emergence of very different and even opposite possibilities. Man can become a wolf or a brother to his fellow man.

(100) When God created man in his image, he endowed him with divine dignity. He fashioned him in his own image and at the same time taught him how to use the earth and its goods for his own good and for the use of

everyone. But as man refused to acknowledge his Lord and Creator and believed that he was his own master, he also destroyed the harmony with himself and his brother and the creatures around him. One of the first major consequences of this discord which entered the world because of Adam's sinfulness and has since served to shape history is the fratricide described in Genesis 4:3 and the following verses.

(101) That is why the Scriptures and the traditions of the Church viewed the history of the faith in Adam as the original delineation of unredeemed man. Jesus Christ is contrasted with him as the origin of a renewed humanity (cf. Rom 5:12–21; 1 Cor 15:21 f.). God himself ordained a new beginning in Jesus Christ by sending his Son. Christ is the new Adam. Our humankind will be renewed in him. Because Jesus Christ took upon himself and redeemed us from the sins of the world, which have always included our own failures, he established a new relationship between man and God the Father, between man and himself and between man and man. By his death and his Resurrection, Jesus Christ tore down the dividing wall of enmity (cf. Eph 2:15 ff.). In this way, man can become a brother to his fellow men through God's devotion in Jesus Christ.

(102) God finally promised and gave us peace in Christ. For that reason, we can overcome evil if our life remains oriented towards God. Our life cannot promote the cause of peace if we leave aside God. In the last analysis, God is a guarantee of peace in that he rouses the conscience of man and inspires him to do good. The promise of peace has to be fulfilled, at least as a beginning and in part, in the concrete circumstances of our life.

(103) However, the Christian faith knows that peace in this world and in this time will always remain under threat and that the presence of God's rule can never be realized completely or in one single design. The final state of peace cannot be achieved in the shape of any new political order. Although the gospel proclaims the presence of God's rule, able to initiate for us our reconciliation with God and among men, the full realization of that rule remains to be brought about under a realm of peace. The old world of sin has not simply disappeared. As the Second Vatican Council taught us, the whole history of mankind is marked by a harsh struggle against the forces of darkness—a struggle which began at the very beginning of the world and which, according to the word of the Lord, will last until the final day (GS 37). Wilfulness and obduracy, self-assertion and arrogance pose a continuous threat to the heart of man. Only in this way can we ultimately understand the universally latent aggressiveness and destructiveness. Even a redeemed man can fall prey to the temptations of power and to the exercise of power in the spirit of self-glorification,

despite the forgiveness of his sins and a new beginning in life after baptism. However, the forces of evil do not only dwell within man himself. Enmity, oppression and violence also loom in the social, political and institutional spheres of our human existence. The willingness to achieve reconciliation and peace must therefore include a sober and vigilant consideration of the treacherous and perfidious nature of evil in the world—otherwise it can easily succumb to the illusions of Lucifer. We must not overlook the drastic situation and the frailty of our world which, despite its redemption, still faces great travail.

(104) For that reason, the Church has always adhered to the necessity of protecting the innocent against brutality and oppression, combating injustice and defending justice and righteousness. As we know from the lessons of history, a universal renunciation of this protection and resistance may be understood as weakness and possibly as an invitation to perpetrate political blackmail. In fact, such a renunciation may foster the very things which it is designed to prevent, namely, the oppression of the innocent and the infliction of suffering and brutality upon them.

(105) This protection is, first and foremost, the task of the government, which can also avail itself of the powers of state—within the limits imposed by the ethical code, law and constitution. Despite the fact that such powers in themselves cannot guarantee a peaceful coexistence among people under the legal system, the ethical legitimacy of their limited and controlled use within the state's sphere of dominion cannot be denied.

(106) As regards external relations, Christian ethics reaffirm the validity of the prohibition of the use of force stipulated by international law, and the prohibition of the threat and use of force. Since the use of force cannot be excluded and, moreover—unlike the internal sphere of rule—no international monopoly of power with the capacity for imposing sanctions really exists, there is no denying a state the right to an ethically permissible defense in certain circumstances. Here, too, the restrictive principle applies that military means cannot by themselves ensure peaceful relations between the nations on the basis of law and righteousness.

(107) For these reasons, the ethical and normative core of the doctrine of a "just defense" retains within a comprehensive peace ethic in the Church a limited function—difficult in specific circumstances but nevertheless hitherto irreplaceable for ethical orientation. This function applies in the peripheral case of a fundamental defense of life and of the freedom of nations when the latter's elementary physical and spiritual substance is threatened or even infringed. However, such an affirmation only possesses justification within the overall context of a peace ethic which

demands the resolute will and the utmost endeavor that everything be done in order to prevent such a situation from supervening. Furthermore, the question of the means of defending such basic human rights of people and nations becomes more and more acute in the age of mass weapons of destruction.

(108) Even though the knowledge and the experience of our frailty form part of the Christian concept of humankind, a Christian cannot satisfy himself with this simple observation. His faith urges him time and time again to display a willingness to further the cause of peace which is not discouraged by disappointments, defeats and contradictions.

(109) It is not a matter of indifference for such actions—which also embrace the sphere of politics—how one regards other people, other nations and other states. Those who are able to see in their adversaries persons of equal value and beings imbued with moral responsibility will always be prepared to meet them half way and to listen to their ideas and aims. Such people will always base their own policies on the "Golden Rule" of the Sermon on the Mount: "Whatsoever you wish that men would do to you, do so to them" (Mt 7:12). Such a peace policy, which is inspired by the precepts of Jesus, concedes to others, including our opponents, the opportunity for making a fresh start and for learning together. In this way, the Christian ethos based on loving one's enemy and practicing nonviolence can—and indeed must—apply in the field of foreign policy and international relations.

(110) Yet that is not enough. The Christian testimony to peace must be verified and supplemented by active service on behalf of that righteousness which alone permits and sustains lasting peace. It is equally an integral part of all Christian actions for peace to champion the elementary rights of every person everywhere and to work everywhere for such living conditions as foster and guarantee his freedom, dignity, and development. The love which Christ taught us by precept and practice enables us to discern the extent of a greater righteousness and to perform unselfish service on its behalf.

(111) Do not these thoughts venture too far from the framework established by God's message? We are convinced that this is not the case. The Sermon on the Mount declared: "Blessed are the peacemakers, for they shall be called children of God" (Mt 5:9). This does not relate to peaceful thoughts, but to the deeds from which peace develops. That means, however, that it accords with the spirit of the Sermon on the Mount when we dispassionately face up to the question as to whether the adoption or omission of certain measures, the provision or non-provision

of certain means, really helps to promote peace and the appropriate conditions for guaranteeing it or whether in fact they place them in jeopardy. With this in mind, we wish in the following chapters to render a contribution to the ethical assessment of measures for promoting and maintaining peace.

4.2 The Promotion of Peace

(112) The promotion and maintenance of international peace is, to begin with, placed within the competence and responsibility of states. But the growing insight into the preconditions of peace, into its social circumstances and the resulting coresponsibility of individuals and of social groups directs us to a much broader responsibility in the social and ethical sphere. Accordingly, the Joint Synod designated peace as "a dynamic process with the threefold goal: firstly, of creating equal chances for a humane development of the individual as well as of all social groups, and equal chances to safeguard such development; secondly, of establishing international and social justice; and thirdly, of building up a community of nations without war" (EF 2.1.2.3). This means that the promotion of peace requires the following:

4.2.1 Respect for Universal Human Rights as Basic Rights

(113) This demand may elicit surprise. Does not the commandment to love one's enemies as demanded by Jesus in his Sermon on the Mount and illustrated by parables invalidate this invocation of the legal standpoint? As God has shown his absolute and unconditional love of man, he must not abandon his love of his fellow men by invoking his right. Love transcends not only one's own legal standpoint; it also goes further than the legal plane of our fellow humans' demands. Nevertheless, it is also true that respect for the rights of our neighbors constitutes a minimum demand in love. This cannot be simply thrust aside. Charity is not a substitute for law. Love even requires, first and foremost, the observance of human rights as the basic rights of every society. The acknowledgment of these rights forms the bridge to peace and freedom, both internally and externally.

(114) It must, then, concern us more and more as we hear and read every day of the multifarious ways in which human rights are trampled on and infringed in different countries. Wherever human rights are violated,

"there is a development of various forms of domination, totalitarianism, neocolonialism and imperialism which are a threat also to the harmonious living together of the nations. Indeed, it is a significant fact, repeatedly confirmed by the experiences of history, that the violation of the rights of man goes hand in hand with violation of the rights of the nation". (*Redemptor Hominis* 17). It is therefore of the utmost importance for promoting peace that we should invariably and everywhere furnish our support in order to ensure the realization of human rights and the changing of systems rooted in injustice. An acceptance of breaches of law and the relativization of one's awareness of the law are tantamount to a strengthening of wrongdoing and violence. A "world without fear" such as the Church has repeatedly demanded will only arise when human rights and international law gain universal recognition which is not circumscribed by the interests of powerful states.

(115) It follows from this for our communal life in a free democracy that we can serve internal and external peace more efficiently, the more fundamental values and basic rights fashion our constitutional conduct. Wherever people live together, there also arise disputes. If everyone regards his viewpoint as correct and that of his adversary as wrong, it is the more powerful or the more cunning, the faster thinking or the more cynical who will prevail. It is the "law of the jungle" which applies. The linking of the power of the state to a basic system founded on human rights fundamentally overcomes this law of the jungle. A democratic state guarantees by dint of its legal system that disputes will be resolved in accordance with agreed rules and above all by independent courts. The division of powers furnishes a safeguard against the abuse of power. The maintenance of peace through law requires the recognition of the law which is equally binding for both parties to the dispute and which safeguards and restricts the freedom of one as well as the other. Let us bear in mind the following:

The right to life. For the Church, the protection of human life is indivisible. Wherever the conviction prevails of the dignity and value of every human being, irrespective of his birth or his achievement in society, that fulfills a fundamental prerequisite for the perception that war can never represent a means of resolving disputes. Let us recall and digest the words of Pope Paul VI when he said that "the killing of a human being, either before or after his birth, infringes above all the inviolable moral principle on which the view of human existence must always rest, namely that the life of man is sacrosanct and holy from the first moment of his conception to the last moment of his natural life in time."[28] The foundations of any legal system are human dignity and the incalculable value of every single person.

The connection between law and freedom. Freedom can only develop wherever law is respected on the basis of fundamental rights. Wherever the awareness of law disappears and breaches of the law are not only officially provoked but also publicly applauded, then both peace and freedom alike are in danger. Those who free themselves from law end up by "freeing" themselves from freedom. On the other hand, law must only restrict the freedom of the individual inasmuch as this is necessary by virtue of the other's right to freedom and of the common good.

The connection between law and equality. Law proceeds from the fundamental equality between all people. It points out to us that everyone must be respected and promoted in equal fashion as a human being. This equality must be realized not only within the framework of our people; it also applies towards other nations and their citizens who live among us. We cannot realize our own identity against the opposition of weaker members of the community, but only with them.

4.2.2 The Promotion of International Justice

(116) The words of Pope Paul VI that "development is the new name for peace" appear to us today as a special challenge. In the public discussion about peace in the world and the world-wide economic crises, we run the danger of classifying this part of our mandate for peace as being of secondary importance.

(117) The situation of the developing countries, to which the so-called "newly industrialized countries" also belong, cannot help but fill us with the most profound concern. Eight hundred million people still live in absolute poverty, hunger and misery. Furthermore, the drastic rise in the cost of energy has increased the debts of the better-off developing nations to an extent which threatens in many cases to bring about state bankruptcy.

(118) In order to build up peace, we must above all remove the causes of discord in the world which lead to war, i.e., primarily the injustices (GS 83). In fact, injustices in the political and economic structures during

[28] Speech on the World Day of Peace 1977. Cf. *AAS* 68 (1976): 707–14 = VAS 23, 164–71.

the last few centuries have served to prevent economically weak countries and their societies from achieving a self-sustained development. The world has not succeeded in allowing a wide section of the population to take part in the developing process, nor has an equal partnership emerged between industrial and developing countries. This condition has worsened recently as a result of the world-wide recession. Furthermore, the contribution by the Eastern bloc to world-wide development aid lags far behind the contributions of the other industrial states. Moreover, nationalism, tribal rivalries and religious fanaticism in many developing countries inhibit development and pose a threat to peace.

(119) However, the matter at stake is no longer solely the crisis in the developing countries. Economic and social problems are also growing apace in the industrial states. Against the background of economic stagnation and a high degree of unemployment, the tendency is growing everywhere to orient oneself towards short-term egotistical interests. Above all, there exists a danger that industrialized countries will hinder imports from developing countries on a wider scale than hitherto. The consequence might be a collapse of world trade, and in that case it would be impossible to avert a universal economic crisis.

(120) In this situation, greater importance than ever now attaches to the much-vaunted interdependence and partnership between industrial and developing countries: It is more necessary than ever to accept joint responsibility for ourselves and for others. A policy oriented towards short-term national interest cannot resolve the world-wide problems. Hunger, unemployment and misery would only grow worse while political instability and warfare would increase to an alarming extent. It is above all important to recognize and to eliminate the manifold causes of this situation:

- the social injustices prevailing in many developing countries;
- the hunger and indigence of a continuously growing number of people;
- the deprivation of human rights and political rights;
- the unjust treatment of minorities;
- the growth of religious and ideological confrontation;
- the injustices within the present world economic system;
- the great arms build-up.

(121) The arms build-up by the developing countries and the resultant hostilities not only cost human lives but also reduce the opportunity of safeguarding a dignified human existence in the forseeable future for a

growing population. Industrial countries and their economic interest are partly to blame for this arms race in the Third World.

(122) The development of the countries of the Third World has become one of the vital issues facing mankind. It has become a special challenge against the background of an arms build-up which costs huge sums. The admonition of the Council applies more than ever: "The arms race is one of the greatest curses on the human race, and the harm it inflicts upon the poor is more than can be endured" (GS 81).

(123) The Church has the task of ensuring that the rights of everyone are preserved in the global trial of strength and that particularly the rights of the poorest members of the community are not trampled underfoot. We cannot satisfy ourselves with a situation whereby the wealthy give up a little of their superabundance to the poor. We must also advocate more justice in the structures of society, for such justice forms the fundament of peace in a world in which everyone has become dependent on everyone else.

(124) The message of Christ which proceeds from the dignity of every individual human being as the image of God is also a message for the liberation of the nations who are struggling to overcome misery, poverty and injustice in their national and international relations.

4.2.3 Development of a World Peace Order

(125) International law forms one of the decisive pillars of world peace. The recognition of its validity sometimes remains dependent on the respect shown to it by the various governments. Every peace system worthy of the name rests ultimately on the justified confidence in the peace-promoting strength of the law. Where this trust is lacking, it remains difficult to fashion reliable international structures of peace which prevent the application of force. Instead, we know from history that powerful states try to impose a "peace order" on their region to serve their own interests. Alternatively, there prevails at best—as at the present time between East and West—a precarious equilibrium of forces which is also neither a "sure or real peace" (GS 81).

(126) The popes of the last seven decades have never tired of calling for a world order of peace. Today, we know more than ever how important it is to have a world order of peace. In a world where everything and everybody is interrelated on a hitherto unknown scale, it has become an urgent ethical commandment. The international organizations have "been the object of attempts at manipulation on the part of nations wishing to

exploit such bodies" in the course of the last few centuries (John Paul II).[29] This must not lead to discouragement and resignation. Instead, we must give fresh thought to the individual structures of the international organization in order to take into account the new realities and conflicts. Every chance must be seized in order to "regain for the organizations the mission which is theirs by virtue of their origin, their charter and their mandate".

(127) In particular, we call for the observance of the prohibition of war and the use of force pursuant to international law and the Charter of the United Nations in particular. It is worthy of notice that, in addition to other states, the Federal Republic of Germany has solemnly affirmed in formal declarations and treaties her renunciation of any use of force and has acted accordingly. The people and the government must continue in their resolution to search for a political, i.e., a peaceful settlement to all such conflicts as may arise.

(128) The Second Vatican Council put forward the proposal that "a universally recognized world authority should be established, possessing adequate power and authority to assure the protection and safety of all, guaranteeing justice and the observation of human rights" (GS 82). Pope Paul VI submitted this proposal in his historic address before the plenary session of the United Nations on October 4, 1965.[30] Such a world authority designed to protect freedom and peace must not be created along the lines of a centralist unitary state. The principle of giving help to those who practice self-help forms the necessary adjunct to the principle of solidarity among all nations. By the same token, the states must be prepared to surrender part of their sovereignty. In order to apply international law we must above all establish a world court of justice whose decisions shall be binding and which will be accompanied by the requisite power of imposing sanctions. Such proposals may appear utopian against the background of the political reality of our times. In the long run, however, there is no alternative way of creating the foundations for a dignified, free and fair coexistence between all nations. Until this goal has been achieved, we must continue to seek interim solutions for safeguarding peace.

---

[29] Speech on the World Day of Peace 1983 (see note 2).
[30] Cf. *AAS* 57 (1965): 885–87 = VAS 23, 52–59.

4.3 The Maintenance of Peace

4.3.1 Security Policy within the Framework of Peace Policy

(129) The discussion about safeguarding peace and freedom is today largely confined to military strategies and arms questions. As a result, the general public gains the impression that peace policy consists above all of security policy. In fact, it cannot be overstressed that peace policy encompasses much more than the efforts simply to safeguard it.

(130) The first principle applicable to the maintenance of peace in the narrower sense of the term—including and indeed especially in East-West relations—consists in what we have already observed in general about the requisite degree of protection against brute force and oppression, about the defense of law and justice and about relations with other states including those of our opponents. There are chiefly two threats looming ahead. The first is the danger to the freedom of nations and their citizens from totalitarian systems which disregard elementary human rights in their sphere of dominion and which might be tempted to use their power for expansion or for the application of political influence and extortion. The second danger lies in an escalation of armaments with an immense accumulation of nuclear and conventional weapons which, as many people fear, might one day cause the catastrophe of an outright war. We must counter both dangers simultaneously—above all by political means.

(131) In the face of the persistent threat from totalitarian systems, citizens are called upon to defend a peace which is governed by respect for human dignity and by concrete freedoms. This defense is not solely or primarily a matter of security policy and military contribution. It requires, first and foremost, a continual confrontation with the ideological basis of Marxism-Leninism at the political, intellectual and moral levels—i.e., a constructive confrontation which bears in mind the foundations of free democratic states and their social system. Moreover, it needs as a reliable foundation a knowledge of the peace-promoting character of law and constitution and the acceptance of these principles. It also necessitates an active and convincing policy for promoting peace. Only in that way can human rights and international law find universal recognition. In this political encounter we can again discern anew the connection between peace and freedom, law and justice as the key to the long-term solution of today's problems.

(132) Nevertheless, this defense cannot forego a military contribution

76

for the time being. In the final analysis, this contribution represents a logical conclusion from the needs created by man's frailty, which renders it necessary to fight injustice. However, an affirmation of military power as a component of security policy does not contradict the enunciated demand of settling conflicts by non-violent methods. Even today, military power must primarily serve this objective. We must therefore consider what demands must be made today of such a military contribution and what criteria should govern it.

(133) In the face of the other danger arising from the arms race, the important thing is to do everything which diminishes the risks of an arms build-up in the interest of our joint survival without endangering one's own security. The threat and use of force must be removed, or at least gradually reduced, in international relations. The methods of non-violence may be considered as acting effectively on the political level when we succeed in introducing and implementing the renunciation of force and the use of non-violent methods for settling disputes in international agreements and treaties.

(134) We have already referred to the necessity for all concerned to develop patterns of behavior oriented towards the "Golden Rule". Dangerous misconceptions and miscalculations can be avoided only if all sides are seriously and permanently willing to reexamine their own position and at the same time to give due consideration to the experience and anxiety, the interests, the perceptions and the values of the other side. Even where fundamental dissent remains in the attitude of individuals and society, it is only on this basis that tension can be reduced while communication and cooperation for one's common benefit can be strengthened.

(135) For this reason, the aim of the military contribution towards the maintenance of peace under present conditions must not lie in the waging of war but in the preventing of war—and indeed of any warfare at all. Armament and military strategy must be judged in the light of this objective and this assessment, and the methods used must also be evaluated in these terms. In view of the weapons of nuclear destruction now available, this fundamental approach acquires a hitherto unknown significance. Concrete issues of strategy, for which there are various evaluations, are highly controversial. Although we have no wish to come forward as arbiters in this dispute, we nevertheless deem it our duty to name criteria for the formation of an opinion.

4.3.2 The Prevention of War

(136) Today, war is less than ever a means of attaining political goals. War must never be allowed to break out! For, the consequences of war have never been so manifest; and never before was it so clear that any possible gain would stand out of all proportion to the sacrifices involved.

(137) This goal of preventing any war at all is no longer a matter of controversy in this country. Be that as it may, everyone—politician and strategist alike—is afflicted by the urgent question of how this goal can be most efficiently and reliably accomplished and how the strategies and means of preventing war must be judged in detail. Pursuant to the general line of thought, the states of the Marxist world are also afraid of a military conflict between the two alliances. Nonetheless, they adhere to the claim of also promoting a revolutionary change of society in every country by violent means. According to the official Leninist doctrine—still not revoked—wars conducted to this end are considered "just wars".

(138) Hitherto, the attempt has been made to prevent war by means of the nuclear deterrent: States threaten each other with consequences in the event of an attack by the other side, consequences which nobody can seriously accept—namely, mutual destruction. The purpose of this strategy of deterrence consists in bringing influence to bear on a potential challenger so that he cannot derive any political or military benefit from a possible aggression. The threat of the deterrent thus serves to prevent an infringement of peace.

(139) The efficacy of this strategy is in dispute. Some people argue that the nuclear deterrent has hitherto prevented the outbreak of hostilities between the two blocs, and that there is no feasible alternative to this strategy for the time being. Others point out that the absence of any war between East and West does not prove that this is the outcome of the deterrent.

(140) At any rate, the following question arises: Under the system of mutual deterrence, can either side really be sure of his opponent's intentions? But as Pope Paul VI affirmed in his message to the first special session of the UN General Assembly devoted to disarmament (1978), "to think that the arms race can thus go on indefinitely without causing a catastrophe would be a tragic illusion".[31] The concomitant dangers of this automatic dynamism in the arms race force us to conclude that nuclear deterrence is not a reliable instrument for preventing war in the long run.

[31] Cf. *AAS* 70 (1978): 399–407 = VAS 23, 176–83.

It is against this background that Pope John Paul II's speech to the second special session of the UN General Assembly devoted to disarmament must be seen. The Pope called upon us to reverse the arms race. He would only tolerate deterrence as a means of maintaining peace along a path which leads to an arms limitation and disarmament: "Under present conditions, dissuasion based on equilibrium—certainly not an end in itself but as a stage on the way to progressive disarmament—can still be judged to be morally acceptable. However, to ensure peace it is indispensable not to be content with a minimum which is always fraught with a real danger of explosion".

(141) This moral toleration of the deterrent—inasmuch as it cannot be immediately renounced without any replacement in order to maintain security along the difficult path leading to disarmament—depends on the fulfilment of very strict conditions which must be all the more strict, the shorter the time at our disposal becomes. With this in mind, let us now try to name some of the standpoints which must be considered in an ethical judgment of the nuclear deterrent.

(142) The first and decisive standpoint is the *goal* of this strategy, i.e., the prevention of war. If that is the goal of the deterrent according to the declared will of politicians and strategists, then the political and military leaders must be able to substantiate the claim that war can really be prevented by this strategy and why they consider this to be the case. Only in that way can one tolerate the enormous risks invariably attendant upon a nuclear arms build-up. This also has a bearing on, for example, the danger in critical situations that political decisions of the utmost significance have to be taken at very short notice by virtue of the nature of the weapons. These and other risks have to be considered in terms of the chance that the nuclear deterrent will force all concerned to enter into negotiations and to settle the dispute by peaceful means. Only where this applies can the political and military leaders earmark the funds and give the soldiers the weapons which, as all most profoundly hope and expect, will never be used. Nevertheless, deterrence must be examined in detail in terms of this objective.

(143) The second standpoint for an assessment of the deterrent thus refers to the *means*, i.e., the envisaged conventional and nuclear weapons as well as the appropriate operational planning. The intention of preventing war with all one's strength must become credible by virtue of the choice of the whole range of arms. The methods chosen to pursue one's security policy should be measured in terms of the goal of preventing war. After all, the possible impact of present and future strategy and tactical

planning as well as the relevant weapons systems on the other side's security policy must be incorporated within the line of thought. Someone who is subject to a potential threat will, in fact, deduce the intention of his opponent to no small extent from the nature of the weapons directed against him. This perception substantially influences the willingness to conduct negotiations. As the experts on peace have emphasized, the arms build-up between East and West is seen, because of one's concept of its threat, against the background of one's own security requirements. However, one must not view specific weapons or systems in isolation from the general context of the strategy to which they relate. If the deterrent is intended to establish above all a political objective for the chosen weapons within the framework of preventing a war, then these weapons must be judged primarily in those terms.

(144) Any assessment of nuclear strategies and nuclear armaments which is made in isolation from this political objective would necessarily lead to a radical condemnation. If the threat to use nuclear weapons is regarded as part of the comprehensive strategy of deterrence with the aim of preventing war, the chances and risks of the threat must be examined with the utmost conscientiousness. Above all, one would have to compare the risk inherent in the mounting uncontrollability of the use of nuclear weapons on the one hand and the danger of the mounting probability of a conventional war on the other.

(145) These various points of view indicate the *criteria* which a deterrence must satisfy if it is still to be acceptable in ethical terms.

– (146) Existing or planned military means must never render war more feasible or more probable.

We clearly realize that this demand of ours will encounter opposition which can scarcely be overcome. After all, weapons only provide an effective deterrent if their use can be threatened in a credible manner. From the standpoint of preventing war, however, the main elements of the strategy of deterrence are the mutual threat of unacceptable levels of destruction and the attendant risk. Precisely the prospect that conventional or nuclear war cannot be limited poses for one's opponent an incalculable risk which is intended to guarantee the mutual deterrent against war—any war. The use of a threat of mass destruction which one must never carry out—a morally intolerable concept—is regarded as being particularly effective for the purpose of preventing war. This immense tension is only acceptable if the whole range of security policy is directed towards the goal of preventing war and if the military measures remain integrated within the higher-ranking concept of maintaining peace by political means.

– (147) Only such military means and so many military means may be deployed as are necessary for the purpose of the deterrent aimed at preventing war.

In particular, the military means must not indicate any quest for superiority. Rather, they must be geared to the objective of achieving stability, which then prevails when neither side can derive political or military benefit from their weapon systems. However, such a restriction in the means of deterrence cannot be the last word on this subject. We must not in the long run satisfy ourselves with a "minimum" of destructive potential, which is "always fraught with a real danger of explosion" (John Paul II). For that reason, all responsible persons in the state and in society have the urgent duty to strive with their whole strength towards finding alternatives to the threat of mass destruction.

– (148) All military means must be compatible with effective mutual arms limitation, arms reduction and disarmament.

If the deterrent—as the Pope said—is to be "a stage on the way to progressive disarmament", the individual military measures must be oriented to credible efforts undertaken to limit and to reduce arms. So far, this goal has not been achieved. It is therefore urgently necessary to introduce a more effective arms control than in the past as the preliminary stage to mutual disarmament. This requires the willingness of both sides. If we are to stop, freeze and finally reverse the arms race, it will be necessary to pursue our own disarmament strategy aimed at reducing still more the mutual threat in favor of cooperative relationships at all levels where these are possible—diplomatic, political, economic and psychological. Such a peace policy presupposes clarity of concepts and the credibility of the people on both sides so that a substantiated trust can arise through the mutual predictability of behavior. A policy of arms reduction must be supplemented by plans for changing over arms production to civilian production.

(149) Similarly, the observance of these criteria does not furnish any absolute guarantee that deterrence reliably prevents war. Many people are therefore concerned about what would happen if the deterrent were to fail and if armed hostilities were to break out. Can weapons designed to deter and to prevent war be meaningfully used in a war pursuant to the principle

81

of the proportionality of the means? Is not the danger of escalation from their use—however limited—so great that one cannot imagine any situation in which one could accept responsibility, after consideration of all factors, to use atomic weapons? In the European sphere, this question also arises in sharper form in the light of the growing destructive power of conventional weapons.

(150) We hope and pray that a situation will never occur in which somebody is confronted with such decision-making. This points once more and with the utmost urgency to the demand that every effort should be made at every political level to prevent hostilities. The renunciation of the threat and use of force in accordance with international law must also be considered as a basis of stability in situations of heightened tension. It is particularly then that communication between both sides must be maintained. For each side must know what the other wants. There must above all be no automatism which emanates from the available weapons systems and proceeds to the decision makers. Particularly in times of crisis, all political decisions must be subject to detailed examination and planning, where possible without any time pressure.

(151) Clearly, the use of atomic weapons or other means of mass destruction for the devastation of population centers or other largely civilian targets can in no circumstances be justified. A war of destruction is never a solution and never permissible. The fact that this possibility nevertheless exists shows that mankind is now in an impasse which forces us to act with courage. The only solution lies in undertaking greater efforts towards a political maintenance of peace and continuous disarmament. States and power blocs must finally learn to shape their relations without the threat or use of force.

4.4 The Hope of Peace

(152) We shall not pass over in silence the fact that our statements, above all on the maintenance of peace, confront us with a great dilemma. On the one hand, we face weapons of mass destruction which have achieved ever greater "perfection" over the years. The use of these weapons would bring upon us a horror that could not be more terrible. That is why we must search more and more urgently, with everyone of good will, for solutions to this problem. On the other hand, we can see quite plainly and without illusion how much injustice, oppression and totalitarian extortion prevail in our world. This, too, is an explosive source of dangers which we must contain so that all people and nations can live in freedom

together. At the same time, we do not overlook the fact that these two sources of danger, however different the causes and the facts may be, are connected with each other and reciprocally augment one another—a situation which many regard as hopeless.

(153) In the light of these circumstances let us name in the present "interim period" (Paul VI)[32] those strict conditions and criteria under which nuclear deterrence can still be tolerated as long as it demonstrably serves to prevent war. By virtue of this decision we are choosing from among various evils the one which, as far as it is humanly possible to tell, appears the smallest. It is the confirmed goal of our efforts, firstly to contribute towards ensuring the prevention of the looming holocaust of mankind and a gradual reduction in the number of weapons of mass destruction, and secondly to strive for a comprehensive system of peace and justice beyond the arsenals of weapons and the systems of oppression.

(154) We are guided in the principles described above by the precept of rationality. At the same time, however, we adhere to the gospel of peace which transcends all our rationality (cf. Phil 4:7) and which leaves far behind all the compromises that are currently necessary. Let us be guided by the words of God, who promises us the peace which this world cannot give by itself (cf. Jn 14.27). It is the resultant tension between promise and de facto circumstances which points to the need for an emergency system while also indicating steps beyond what is now possible. We believe that "with God all things are possible" (Mt 19:26). Those who rely on this will never be able to accept the existing conditions (cf. Mk 9:23). Such people are summoned to hope against hope (cf. Rom 4:18).

4.4.1 Promise and Reality

(155) We speak from our faith in God, who anticipated our wishes in Jesus Christ. He manifests his love and loyalty towards us by seeking reconciliation with us when we were still sinners and enemies (Rom 5:6–11; 2 Cor 5:19–21). "He makes his sun rise on the evil and on the good" and reveals himself in his liberating love for his enemies (Mt 5:43–48). He invites us to pursue a path along which he himself has come towards us—a path marked by creative nonviolence, immense willingness to forgive and unswerving love of one's enemies. This greater righteousness of God (Mt 5:20) is the origin and criterion of Christian hope and action. From this righteousness springs the faith and tranquillity (Mt 6:25–34) which transcends all rational thought about security—that

[32] Speech on the World Day of Peace 1983 (see note 2).

disarming love which Jesus himself experienced before he called upon others to do likewise. We resist the temptation to indulge in resignation and illusions, even if these seem very near at hand. We have firm confidence that the logic of the arms race will be overcome. We believe in God as the only Lord of history. We know from the gospel that this emergency situation is not the final word in worldly wisdom, for God's wisdom is not our wisdom.

(156) We find ourselves being summoned all the more as Christians to realize the patterns of behavior and forms of life which testify here and now to God's greater justice. We must not and we do not want simply to react. On the contrary, we endeavor on the basis of our faith to become active ourselves and to accept the alternatives in the gospel literally. Christian endeavors on behalf of peace include the advocacy of the kingdom of God, readiness for reconciliation, protest and non-violent resistance against injustice within the limits of the law. Christian endeavor on behalf of peace signifies loving our enemies, making sacrifices, laying down our own life. We must prepare now for that order of peace which does not require any threat of force for its protection, but which rests on mutual trust and justice. This necessitates courage to rethink one's position and to reverse it. The establishment of potentials of power and the demonstration of power cannot as such constitute a political goal for Christians.

4.4.2 Encouragement to Take the Next Steps

(157) We adhere to the "greater righteousness" of the gospel as the criterion for our faith. But have we already sufficiently understood and realized the promises and demands of the Sermon on the Mount? Have we already exhausted their content of hope and their scope for action? Are we overcoming evil by goodness (cf. Mt. 5:39, Rom 12:21)? Our testimony to peace is in fact only credible when we take every possible step, including the smallest of steps, in the direction of peace.

(158) In the international relations between states, the urge to expand and achieve predominance and the ruthless exploitation of our own advantages at the expense of others contradict God's will and the wish for survival by mankind, which can only resolve its problems in partnership and solidarity. It is therefore important, apart from one's own security, to incorporate the security of our opponents into our considerations. Wherever economic superiority and predominance exist, as between North and South, then we must strengthen the weaker partners so that

they can avail themselves of the same rights and duties. Wherever oppression and extortion loom, it is important to promote the right to self-determination and self-development free from the use of power and the wish for revenge. We must also assign great importance to economic and academic exchanges for the benefit of both sides. A free flow of people across borders and a free exchange of information and opinions serve to establish a just order of peace.

(159) Anyone who thinks only of himself and looks to his own advantage must realize that, in the long term, he is only damaging himself. In order to strengthen confidence in international relations, we must take into account the possibility of advance concessions, provided that these do not endanger our security and legitimate self-interests. Together with the Pope, we encourage our responsible politicians to take "all steps, even the smallest ones, of reasonable dialogue in this very important sphere" (Pope John Paul II).[33] Those who do not take possible and therefore necessary steps towards promoting peace and those who do not make full use of the opportunities for cooperation and fundamentally deny other governments and nations any capacity for learning how to settle their disputes in a non-violent manner are not only neglecting a chance of reducing the use of force but are also, in view of our threatening situation in the world, offending in a culpable manner against the future of the living and of future generations.

(160) In interpersonal relations, the path leading to peace is often blocked by deep-seated anxieties and the resultant will to power. From one's own lack of security, there springs an aggressive need for security; our fellow humans become competitors, opponents and finally enemies. Those who endeavor to find themselves and their fellow men through their faith in God will behold the beam in their own eye (Mt 7:3). Those who see themselves and others within the given possibilities and limits in a spirit of courage, patience and empathy will always endeavor to reach an understanding and forgiveness.

(161) In the life of our congregations and in relations between Christians and their Church, the essential thing is to testify to those matters which serve peace. Particularly in those areas where conflicts have to be resolved and divisions overcome, the spirit of reconciliation and forgiveness wishes to prove good. It is therefore of special importance for our service on behalf of peace and the credibility of that service to conduct a dialogue within the Church and between the churches. The more that we as

---

[33] Speech on the World Day of Peace 1975, cf. *AAS* 67 (1975) 61–67 = V AS 23, 143–49.

Christians and members of the Church give practical expression to the promises and demands of the Sermon on the Mount, the more this will give rise to exemplary forms of behavior and also convince others and appeal to them.

(162) The important thing is for us to strengthen the capacity of the Church to promote peace. In many countries, the Church is a vital force and rooted in the people; she lives in the community between all local churches and in international links and she possesses in the person of the pope a common leader who can speak on behalf of the world Church. The Church can become, more than hitherto, the future model for a world society in freedom and justice by virtue of the manner in which churches behave towards each other in all countries and continents both internally and externally, the manner in which the internal ecclesiastical dialogue is promoted and the conflicts resolved and the manner in which the Church shapes her relationship with society. Admittedly, this can only be successful to the extent that we all can be converted once more to the imitation of our Lord Jesus Christ.

5. IMPULSES AND RECOMMENDATIONS ON WORK FOR PEACE

(163) When we as Christians speak of peace, we are speaking of more than simply the peace which can be maintained, safeguarded, endangered or destroyed in political or military terms. We are speaking of the peace which is greater than everything that we can imagine, plan and achieve (cf. Phil 4:7), the greater peace. At the same time, however, we are also speaking of something which is much closer to our experience and deeds than the peace which constitutes a direct political task—namely, the peace which begins in our hearts and exists between us in everyday life, the closer peace.

(164) The fact that, out of a sense of Christian responsibility, we must not withdraw from service on behalf of that peace which determines relations between states and nations that are free from force, threat and extortion—that is something which inspires our thoughts on promoting and maintaining peace. The prospect of the greater peace which God can give us beyond any human standard of measurement and the efforts on behalf of the closer peace which must begin every day afresh among us personally and between us personally meanwhile bear a decisive relationship to the political peace between states. Without the more long-term perspective, the passion for peace between states and nations lacks the

strength which inspires us never to abandon the process of laborious small steps and to press ahead despite setbacks.

(165) Without this closer approach to peace in our own hearts and in everyday life, peace in the world lacks the net which supports it and which acts as a safeguard. The greater measure of hope and the smaller scale of action also open up our hearts for participation, particularly in the political tasks of a comprehensive service on behalf of peace.

(166) The greater, and therefore the closer, peace of God can never be so personally and effectively felt as in the celebration of the Eucharist. In the Eucharist we ask for and we receive the peace of Christ and the peace which Christ in our midst represents. In the Eucharist, the peace of Christ is proclaimed to us. In the Eucharist, we are sent out to do service on behalf of peace. In this way, the Eucharist forms the three fundamental tasks of the Church and of every Christian:

– to celebrate the peace given by God in the liturgy, to thank God for peace and to beseech him time and time again to grant us peace;
– to proclaim "the gospel of peace" (Eph 6:15), to fashion the conscience of mankind according to the glad tidings of peace and to testify to this peace before the world;
– to render service to peace in the Church, in society and in the state.

5.1 Asking for Peace

(167) In their meeting with Jesus Christ as the fundamental sacrament of the peace of God, Christians now receive God's peace—admittedly in rudimentary form, yet nevertheless really and effectively. This peace is not only a peace of the heart in which Christians believe themselves to be reconciled with God. In his peace, God also shows people a new side of each other as brothers and sisters who appeal to God as their Father. From this experience, Christians assure themselves of the staunch hope that peace in the world is possible despite the apparent contradiction of so much discord in existence.

(168) In the Eucharist, Christians observe the mystery of the death and the Resurrection of Jesus, through which there was bestowed upon them, once and for all, reconciliation with God and with mankind. This event at Easter represents the abandonment of the paths of evil which lead away from God as well as from each other. In the intercessions, we voice to God our current needs and the problems of discord. Even though differing experience and convictions are not intended to be thrust aside, there is nevertheless no place in divine worship for political disputation and

ideological strife. By dint of the forgiveness of sins at the altar, the peace which Christ gave from his sacrifice on the Cross becomes reality. At the sign of peace, Christians pass on to each other the gift of peace. In the celebration of the Eucharist, God invites us to take our places at his table. The meal together is an original symbol of peace in which the faithful overcome whatever separates them. The Church becomes an empirical entity as a community of faith which transcends states and nations— particularly when Christians from other countries share in our celebration and shaping of the liturgy.

(169) The Eucharist and Sunday form one unit. For that reason, Sunday gives us a prior idea of the eternal peace which the Lord of the world will grant us when he returns. Therefore, Christians celebrate Sunday as the continuously recurring day of peace.

(170) Prayers for peace hold their central place in the life of the individual Christian and in the life of the congregation. What Christians ask for is, in fact, the blessing of God. In the comprehensive sense of the word, the blessing signifies incorporation within the divine order of the world. The blessing of God thus means that all human activity acquires its point from him. Our prayers to the Lord and the celebration of peace in the Eucharist which also prepares everyday Christian life for peace are not a pious adjunct or a religious exaggeration but an effective part of service on behalf of peace: These are, in essence, the only approach towards overcoming anxiety, distrust and enmity. We must clearly acknowledge how small and hopeless our own contribution to peace remains when we consider it on its own.

(171) Prayer contains the roots of the spiritual and moral strength of the reawakening needed by the world in order to take decisive steps towards peace. Worship on behalf of peace and pilgrimages of peace are appropriate manifestations for a community of Christians. The daily prayer to the Angel of the Lord, which our ancestors spoke as their prayer of peace in times of danger, can also serve today as the regular call to prayer on behalf of peace. We ask the Virgin Mary, the Queen of Peace, in the prayer of the Rosary as well as in other prayers, to intercede on our behalf. In the intercessions, we also think of our opponents, for prayer for them is a special expression of the love of one's enemies.

(172) We call upon families, congregations and associations to agree on communities of prayer with a family, a parish or an association abroad so that, for example, prayers are said on the first Sunday of every month at the same time in a church in Poland and in a church in our country for the peace of the world. The ecumenical crossroads between the youth of the

German Democratic Republic and the Federal Republic of Germany already furnishes such an example.

(173) But because Christians often fail in conflicts and present the world with a picture of discord, it becomes necessary again and again to turn back from our former ways and to do penance. In the sacrament of penance, the infringed peace with God is restored by the service of the Church. Liturgies of penance, hours of silence and days of fasting impart a credible expression to the concept of doing penance. A Friday of sacrifices on the day when our Lord died and the times of penance during the Church year can promote peace in the Church and thus also become signs of peace for the world.

(174) The service rendered by the Church on behalf of peace is not confined to requests to God to grant us peace. Whatever God gives to the Church is something which the Church must also testify to before mankind.

5.2 Proclaiming Peace

(175) The Church ought to present this peace, which is Christ, by virtue of her deeds and her existence. In every proclamation of peace, she must manifest this peace of Christ. The fact that the Christian message is the "gospel of peace" (Eph. 6:15) must find expression in the sermons and catechesis. In this way, the Church opens up the hope which does not disappoint; she inspires a change of heart without which peace does not grow; and she indicates paths to a new beginning which makes for peace on both a small and a large scale.

(176) It is only the word which has become flesh and life which moves and convinces us. The Church must never renounce the proclamation of peace, just as we must never renounce a life based on that proclamation. Christians are called upon to manifest peace by virtue of their life, their manner and their appearance. This is not possible without acceptance of themselves. So many people are not reconciled to their existence and their fate. They find it difficult to accept their conditions of life, their past and their future. But all of us have already been accepted, and thus we can accept ourselves, too. Wherever such acceptance does not take place and does not penetrate externally, there remains an uneliminated potential for tension and discord between people.

(177) Self-acceptance is not possible without acceptance of each other: We must accept each other just as Christ has accepted us (cf. Rom 15:7). The basis and the scale of this acceptance is the love of Christ, who gave

his life for us. Peace presupposes *reconciliation*. In our imitation of Jesus Christ, we are called upon to make the first step towards our brother or sister and to extend our hand in reconciliation: "First be reconciled to thy brother" (Mt 5:24). We know how often Christians fail, particularly in this field, and thus obscure the gospel of Christ. It is not possible to achieve peace without changing standpoints and patterns of conduct which proceed on the basis of our own personality and our personal interests more than that of our neighbor and his interests and more than on the basis of the whole and the common good. An alteration of our perspective so that we do not look at others from our point of view but at ourselves from their point of view possesses fundamental importance for everyone and in particular for Christians. What we have to learn and to practice are the methods of peace such as learning a new form of expression which tells the truth in love so that others can understand themselves and me, too, learning to listen before speaking, and learning to incorporate the views and interests of others, without which a clash of opinions is inevitable.

(178) In other words, service on behalf of peace begins with a comprehensive education for peace which helps to arouse and to develop, time and time again, the willingness and the ability to maintain peace. It must become clear for Christians in their interrelationships that they can respect each other and speak frankly with each other even though they hold different opinions. Such a frank and unprejudiced discussion about issues of peace will not endanger the internal peace of a group or a community.

(179) The first place for such an education for peace is the family. What is begun here must continue in groups and associations, in youth welfare work and in religious teaching. We particularly ask women and mothers to help in this sphere. They are, to a particular degree, the "intermediaries of reconciliation in the families and in society" (Paul VI).[34] Teaching at school must not mislead children and adolescents into adopting a friend-or-foe way of thinking. Education in peace always militates against the ideologies of conflict which intensify strife and dispute among mankind. At the same time, one should not deny the existence of disputes and differences of opinion; these must be resolved honestly in a manner which promotes peace instead of endangering it.

(180) Youth and adult education also has a role to play in the fundamental formation of judgment and conscience. The help of experienced instructors, psychologists and politicians, peace researchers and military

[34] Cf. in particular the memorandum of the Office for Public Responsibility of the Evangelical Church in Germany, *Frieden wahren, fördern und erneuern*, (Gütersloh, 1981).

experts also has a big role to play. More than anything else, it is necessary to deepen the awareness of the Church's doctrine of peace as set out in the pronouncements of the popes, the documents of the Second Vatican Council and the resolutions of the Joint Synod of Bishops in the Federal Republic of Germany. We also recommend a study of the papal messages on the World Days of Peace and the relevant background material. Their treatment of certain themes offers a good introduction to individual aspects of peace and the work on behalf of peace.

(181) Pope John Paul II has stressed on many occasions the importance of ecclesiastical work in the formation of public conscience and awareness of matters of peace and of human rights. As the Joint Synod stressed, the associations and special committees as well as the congregations and holders of public appointments have differing tasks and responsibilities. The special competence of the political bodies is not curtailed by Church activities to promote peace; it is in fact reaffirmed (cf. EF 2.2.2). The ministers of the Church are expected to proclaim the principles and norms of the ethical code on matters of peace, however convenient or inconvenient this may be. In this way, an orientation for present and future action is furnished for the conscience of the faithful and for all people of good will. The responsibility for the application of moral principles is borne by the person concerned himself, and it cannot be removed from his shoulders.

(182) In our service to promote peace, we know that we have the close support of all Christian churches and Christian communities,[35] together with all courageous peacemakers who work in the spirit of the gospel of Jesus Christ. In the awareness of their common responsibility for peace, Catholic Christians work with Christians of other denominations, with those of other faiths, with unbelievers and with all people of good will.

(183) We attach great importance to the dialogue between young persons and adults. Both groups have a different horizon of experience and can therefore pass on fresh knowledge to each other. Many young people throughout the world today reveal a new awareness of the world-wide human community which transcends all frontiers. They are moving towards a mental outlook stamped by love of justice and willingness to make a personal effort free from either scepticism or cowardice.

(184) Nevertheless, the attitude to life among quite a number of young persons is also characterized by fear and hopelessness. That is why we call upon the generation of adults to pass on their experience to young persons

[35] "Communio et Progressio" pastoral instruction on the instruments of social communication, in *Nachkonziliare Dokumentation* (Trier, 1971), vol. 11.

and to open up opportunities for young men and women to assume a measure of responsibility. Only in this way can we succeed in breathing life and substance into the rules of freedom and law and democracy so that they will also appear attractive and worthwhile for future generations. We appeal to young persons: Do not withdraw from the responsibility which has been thrust upon you! Decide to cooperate in the spheres of life in which you stand! In your discussions of the various aspects of peace policy, aspire to a dialogue with experts and decision makers! Do not be disappointed if you do not achieve swift results, but continue to work persistently on behalf of peace! But do not be misled by false slogans about peace which pretend to aspire to peace but which simultaneously promote hatred, enmity and violence!

(185) Whether or not somebody really wishes to serve the cause of peace or to pursue quite different objectives may be recognized by whether he speaks the language of peace or whether he foments hatred and contempt and adheres to egotistical interests. Peace among mankind and among the nations presupposes that we know of each other and that we know our given circumstances of life. The media count among "the most effective forces and opportunities" for achieving understanding and settlement. These "establish contacts among people" and create "a new language" (*Communio et Progressio* 12).[36] The decision-makers in the media thus bear great responsibility in the efforts towards achieving a permanent peace. The quality of their work largely decides what chances the general public will possess to comprehend the world of today and, on the basis of this comprehension, to act in a manner likely to promote peace.

(186) Finally, Christians can testify to their promotion of peace along the lines of the gospel by an attitude of mind which transcends the bounds of what is customary. Let us turn aside from paths which are not the paths of faith: an inordinate degree of consumption at the expense of the poor, acceptance of selfish life-styles under an exaggerated philosophy of excessive affluence, a demanding mentality circumscribed solely by one's own interests.

(187) Our work for peace must not be confined to words and fine gestures. If our Christian testimony is to be credible in the eyes of the world, it must also be reaffirmed by deeds which serve the cause of peace.

---

[36] Cf. for example the *Studien des katholischen Arbeitskreises Entwicklung und Frieden*, by the German Commission on Justice and Peace, Entwicklung und Frieden (Mainz and Munich).

5.3 Living for Peace

(188) The "gospel of peace" inspires us Christians to live a life of peace and indeed to live for peace. We wish to refer to a number of spheres in which we bear special responsibility as Christians.

5.3.1 Dialogue

(189) As we stressed at the beginning, Pope John Paul II in his message on the 1983 World Day of Peace described dialogue as the path of peace and as the path to peace. Particularly in the present public argument about peace, we consider it very important to respect the rules of dialogue. To this end, the dialogue on behalf of peace should proceed at all levels in the Church and in society. The fact that individual ecclesiastical groups and institutions are concerned with the various aspects of peace is a matter which deserves acknowledgment and recognition. Nonetheless, it is necessary for the whole people of God, in their unity about the fundamental questions of peace, to arrive at more profound perceptions and to find the motivation for fresh deeds.

(190) Let us continue the comprehensive dialogue on the ethics of peace with the Holy Father and with the bishops of other countries in order to discern more clearly what has to be done. These contacts are particularly important and necessary in the case of those nations whose relations with us are impaired by the past.

(191) It is our wish that theological research and teaching will deal more intensively with the fundamental problems of peace, its fulfillment in today's political reality and the practical contributions which the Church can make.[37]

5.3.2 Human Rights

(192) One of the ways of promoting peace is to support the realization of human rights and to resist their violation everywhere in an effective manner.

(193) The central bodies and institutions of the Church will submit, on a

---

[37] Cf. the report on the fifth symposium of the Council of the European Bishops' Conferences in Rome (October 4–8, 1982), *Die kollegiale Verantwortung der Bischöfe und Bischofskonferenzen Europas in der Evangelisierung des Kontinents*, Stimmen der Weltkirche no. 16, issued by the Secretariat of the German Bishops' Conference.

regular basis, documents and reports on infringements of human rights as well as infringements of the right to freedom of religion. We call upon the congregations and the associations to obtain the relevant information and to use their best endeavors within the framework of their possibilities to ensure that human rights are observed. We recommend that the subject of human rights should be again placed on repeated occasions on the agenda of the committees on "mission, development and peace" at the various levels down to the parishes as well as in the associations.

(194) We call upon the journalists and the editors in the media to make a greater contribution in their work towards ensuring that the citizens of our country do not unfeelingly accept the violation of human rights and the use of force everywhere in the world. We call upon those with positions of responsibility in the business world and in politics always to see to it during their negotiations with their partners that the observance of human dignity is not sacrificed to the fulfillment of short-term interests.

5.3.3 Services for Peace

(195) More than in the past, the movement for peace should concentrate on combating the causes of disputes and not adhere to criticism of their consequences. The popes have never tired during recent decades of repeatedly emphasizing that the promotion of peace is a much greater and more significant task than the maintenance of peace.

(196) We are grateful to know that the Church in Germany has become active in this sphere in a whole series of works and initiatives. We need only refer to the great activities of ADVENIAT, MISEREOR and MISSIO, the CARITAS Association, the Commission Justitia et Pax and the European Aid Fund. The Catholic conferences have also dealt more and more with these questions. Mention should also be made here of the initiatives undertaken by the Catholic associations for refugees and expellees directly after the Second World War and the contributions by Pax Christi towards reconciliation with France and Poland. They all placed themselves at the disposal of the social "Diakonia", of the mission, of development and peace.

(197) The Joint Synod had already stressed the importance of institutionalized voluntary services which, according to their understanding of their role, are specifically directed towards promoting peace (EF 2.2.4). These voluntary services can be performed in the sphere of development aid, social projects abroad or social work in our own country. We

welcome the willingness of many young persons to render voluntary service. We shall support all appropriate initiatives which give young persons in particular the possibility of concretely and effectively translating their commitment to peace into deeds. It would be a good thing if the state would attach greater importance to its own services and to social services primarily designed to strengthen the cause of peace.

(198) We emphatically repeat the principle which the Joint Synod also enunciated: "Insofar as the individual services for peace concur in their aims and aspire to the world-wide maintenance and promotion of peace, it can be said that they mutually influence and supplement each other along their various avenues leading to this goal" (EF 2.2.4.5).

(199) *Military Service and Civilian Service.* We would like to direct a special message to all those who render military or civilian service. The safeguarding and promoting of peace constitute central tasks in politics. The development of international relations between East and West which lead to the security problems and their ethical implications set out in the declaration mentioned above lead us to the question as to what criteria should apply to an ethical assessment of military service and refusal to perform combat duties or civilian service.

(200) In this context, we must begin by referring to the remaining dilemma of all service on behalf of peace. The difference between the promise and the fulfilment of peace and the conditions of this time in world history still persists. It also exercises an impact upon those who render a specific service. A soldier who serves in order to safeguard peace must withstand the tension of knowing that he is arming himself on behalf of the state, preparing to fight and learning to do something which he hopes that he will never have to perform, because there is nothing that he desires more resolutely than to preserve peace without the use of force and to resolve conflicts by means of negotiation.

(201) Those who refuse to perform military service for reasons of conscience have also to live to an equal extent with another strain: If everyone were to follow their example, this would create a vacuum of power which can lead to vulnerability to political blackmail, something which they certainly wish to avoid. Moreover, the military services which they themselves cannot render may possibly permit a peaceful settlement of disputes which they too support in freedom and for which they perhaps also demonstrate.

(202) With regard to military service, let us recall the words of the Second Vatican Council that "all those who enter the military service in

loyalty to their country should look upon themselves as the custodians of the security and freedom of their fellow countrymen; and when they carry out their duty properly, they are contributing to the maintenance of peace" (GS 79). If and as long as security policy pursues ethically permissible and indeed obligatory goals—prevention of war, defense of ethical and political values against totalitarian threats and the promotion of disarmament—and avails itself in this of ethically acceptable methods and means, then the service rendered by soldiers is both indispensable and morally justified.

(203) On this basis, we acknowledge the mandate and the service of soldiers in the German Armed Forces. The state, society and also the Church rely on soldiers performing their duties with expert skill and personal courage. The soldier makes a personal contribution to service on behalf of peace by a keen awareness of his moral responsibility to perform that service. Participation in the formation of political and ethical opinions and judgments represent an expression of his awareness of responsibility.

(204) Those who, faced by the dilemma inherent in the safeguarding of peace, refuse war service for reasons of conscience and perform civilian service are also promoting peace—particularly if they furnish creative initiatives such as by their service to the disabled and the fringe groups of society (cf. EF 2.2.4.3). We know how effective this service is and we acknowledge their efforts.

(205) It is gratifying to note the decrease in many prejudices between the various groups of those performing service during the last few years. We urgently call upon all concerned to aspire to a common debate in accordance with the rules of dialogue in the congregations and associations, to respect the various convictions and to subject themselves jointly to the ethical issues in the light of Church teachings on peace.

5.3.4 Development Activities

(206) The discord which becomes manifest in the arms build-up and which particularly concerns us in this letter must not—and we have repeated this elsewhere—superimpose itself upon the other disputes accruing from the lack of justice between North and South. Particularly in times of great international economic difficulties, development policy and development aid cannot always be made available. But in no case should the price of economic security lie in increased exports of arms. People in the North and South require perspectives which go beyond the state budget for the next few years. Moreover, they are calling more and more

urgently for a situation whereby development is not confined to building up economic relations and structures but includes an interflow of cultural exchange. We Christians know about the fresh impulses for our ecclesial life which we owe to our brothers in Africa, Latin America and Asia.

5.3.5 The Unity of Europe

(207) We all expect the fulfilment of European unity to make progress. At her best times, Europe was always a religious, spiritual and cultural unit. There has to be a detailed examination of what can be done to promote this spiritual unity of Europe beyond the present limits, which are apparently insuperable in political terms. As the results of the symposium of the Council of the European Bishops' Conferences in Rome in 1982 have shown, the Church has an important contribution to render.[38] The catholicity of our Church can be expressed by congregations and associations carrying on a partnership with a congregation or an association in another country of Europe. In the case of those cities which already entertain partnerships at the political level, we recommend that the Church congregations take part in these contracts. In this way, the world Church will become a living and exemplary experience. Particularly with Poland, the contacts between the two churches have strengthened to a gratifying degree such as nobody would have deemed possible even a few years ago; this applies especially at the present time of affliction. We would also recall the European pilgrimage movement and call upon the faithful to seize this opportunity.

(208) The cohesion of Europe is also promoted or hindered by the manner in which we deal with our foreign fellow citizens. In the congregations where fellow citizens with a different mother tongue live, we recommend that meetings be organized between Germans and foreigners and that working groups or neighborhood initiatives for assistance should deal with their special problems. Especially in the current situation, marked by economic difficulties, we beseech all Christians to manifest solidarity with their fellow citizens from abroad and to counteract latent or manifest unfriendliness towards foreigners. In this way, we can realize peace immediately on our own doorstep.

(209) When seemingly insuperable disputes have arisen between social groups, peoples and states, it is essential to take the first step, to be the first in asking for forgiveness and to aspire to a compromise. Christians— including those expelled from their homelands who, even at an early

---

[38] Cf. *Charta der Heimatvertriebenen*, August 5, 1950.

stage, expressly renounced revenge and offered reconciliation—have been able to make a contribution (especially in Poland, France and Germany) to initiating a spirit of forgiveness and reconciliation between the sorely tried peoples of Central Europe. These efforts must be continued to an even greater extent vis-à-vis our Eastern neighbors and chiefly towards those who, during this period, have had to accept bondage and the disappointment of many hopes in a painful manner.

5.3.6 Political Responsibility

(210) It is the task of all citizens to promote and maintain peace. Individuals, families, groups, associations, parties and social organizations, political bodies and institutions, governments and international organizations—they all have, in their respective ways, a role to play in realizing peace. Each person ought to assume political responsibility in accordance with his given opportunities. The discharge of such responsibilities must be guided by moral criteria such as we have set out following the teachings of the gospel. The internal and external peace of a society must not be placed at risk. Christians must show special respect for democratically legitimated majority decisions based on justice and law. That holds particularly true of cases where they do not agree in a specific instance with one's personal judgment. Groups and initiatives which feel the decisions taken by the politicians to be wrong must repeatedly examine whether the methods chosen for their complaint or protest constitute a credible testimony to their Christian will for peace. We call upon you to select such avenues of approach of which you can justifiably claim that they will remain non-violent, that they are committed to the fundamental values of our constitutional law and that they will not lead to illegal acts.

(211) Finally, we ask all readers of this letter to work together with us for the cause of peace. We realize that we are unable to offer any complete solutions. Nevertheless, the precepts given by the popes and the Second Vatican Council indicate the direction which we must continue to pursue. We have not been able to express our views on many individual questions, but we shall make further efforts to find the right avenues of approach. All men and women are summoned to take part in the dialogue for peace and the service for peace.

(212) The Holy Year of Redemption which Pope John Paul II inaugurated a few weeks ago is intended to become a year of penance and of

prayer for peace. The following prayer has been handed down to us in the spirit of St. Francis:

> *Lord, make me an instrument of your peace. Where there is hatred, let me sow love; where there is doubt, faith; where there is despair, hope; where there is darkness, light; and where there is sadness, joy.*
>
> *O divine Master, grant that I may not so much seek to be consoled as to console, to be understood as to understand, to be loved as to love; for it is in giving that we receive, it is in pardoning that we are pardoned, and it is in dying that we are born to eternal life.*

WINNING THE PEACE

JOINT PASTORAL LETTER OF THE FRENCH BISHOPS

(1) The specter of a third World War once again haunts our minds. Some years of relative detente, without slowing down the arms race, have lowered the fever of war throughout the world. But the events in Poland, the invasion of Afghanistan, the installation of SS-20 rockets in Eastern Europe and the project aimed at readjusting the balance of armaments by means of the Pershing missiles have revived the fear everywhere and also revived pacifist demonstrations in the West.

(2) Humanity is reaching a frightening threshold, and people are well aware of it: A nuclear conflict would destroy the planet. War is no longer a means of settling conflicts—if it ever had been! "Justice, then, right reason and consideration for human dignity and life urgently demand that the arms race should cease" (as John XXIII wrote in the encyclical *Pacem in Terris*).[1] Yet violence and oppression exist: Would not an unconditional refusal to defend oneself provide an opportunity for blackmail? A nuclear war would annihilate the earth, but is it necessary, for the sake of saving the peace, to give up our liberty, our dignity? Can we envisage a defense which stands below the nuclear threshold? Is "the non-violent alternative" commensurate to the threat? How do we find a way out from this labyrinth in which all of humanity risks being destroyed? No one can any longer escape this question.

(3) In the name of the Lord, source of the life which he has conferred upon men, the Church must recall in season and out of season his plan and design of love and reconciliation. "The Church is guardian of the heritage of the divine Word and draws religious and moral principles from it, but she does not always have a ready answer to every question. Still, she is eager to associate the light of revelation with the experience of mankind in trying to clarify the course upon which mankind has just entered" (*The Church in the Modern World*, 33, 2).

(4) This is why, after lengthy exchanges with competent people of

[1] No. 112.

every persuasion, the bishops of many countries have recently published documents—sometimes rich in content—in order to assist men in exploring new approaches by means of the light of faith. As for ourselves, we would merely wish to make our contribution as pastors of the Church of Jesus Christ, to the universal effort aimed at the construction of authentic peace.[2]

I. BETWEEN WAR AND BLACKMAIL

War

(5) The threat of nuclear conflict is not illusory. The suicidal nature of such a conflict makes it improbable but not impossible. Experts doubt the possibility of controlling it and of limiting it if it ever is unleashed. No one would win a nuclear war. It would be the suicide of humanity. Both superpowers have the wherewithal to annihilate one another seven times over: Would their allies and the "nonaligned" be able to escape this overkill? Moreover, the specialists call the last stage of a nuclear war "nuclear madness".[3] No reason could ever justify the unleashing of such a conflagration, since the survival of humanity is at stake. The same can be said for other forms of suicidal warfare about which less is said, even though preparations are being made: bacteriological (germ) and chemical warfare. However, by paying too much attention to nuclear warfare, we can risk minimizing "conventional" modern forms of warfare. More "controllable" (and thereby less totally immoral), a classical type of warfare tends also to become madness: The bombings of Tokyo, of Dresden, or of Hamburg have produced more victims than both atomic bombs at Hiroshima and Nagasaki, and everyone knows that, in a direct confrontation between two nuclear powers using conventional arms, classical armaments would risk being a detonator for tactical nuclear

---

[2] Cf. Vatican II, *The Church in the Modern World*, no. 33, 2: "In the face of this immense enterprise now involving the whole human race men are troubled by many questionings. What is the meaning and value of this feverish activity? How ought all of these things be used? To what goal is all this individual and collective enterprise heading? The Church is guardian of the heritage of the divine Word and draws religious and moral principles from it, but she does not always have a ready answer to every question. Still, she is eager to associate the light of revelation with the experience of mankind in trying to clarify the course upon which mankind has just entered."

[3] Cf. Herman Kahn, *De l'escalade, metaphore et scenario* (Paris: Calmann-Levy, 1966), 231.

weapons, then strategic nuclear weapons. It would be difficult for a power possessing nuclear arms not to have recourse to them if it believed itself to be at a disadvantage because of conventional armaments. This is why the nuclear powers have very carefully avoided, up to now, confronting one another directly.

(6) Twenty years ago the Second Vatican Council declared: "All these factors force us to undertake a completely fresh reappraisal of war."[4]

Blackmail

(7) Frankly, no one wants war—least of all the specialists, better informed about the risks at stake. The "victor" (?) would find himself ruined, and the advantage of ruling over a "pulverized" adversary is not all that evident. Some countries are very well-skilled at seizing the advantages of war without paying the price of its having been unleashed: Simply by fomenting the threat of war, they commit permanent blackmail. Hitler used this strategy with the Western democracies. They avoided any action rather than provoke him on the occasion of the rearmament of the Ruhr, the occupation of Austria, then of the Sudetenland, and finally of the whole of Czechoslovakia. It took the invasion of Poland to make them realize that they had postponed the inevitable. "The conqueror always loves peace. He would wish to penetrate our territory without meeting resistance", Clausewitz, a specialist in this matter, once wrote. [Karl von Clausewitz (1780–1831), a Prussian general and noted writer on military strategy. His famous book on war advocated "total warfare" against every possible target, including children and private property. "War is the conduct of politics by other means." —Tr.]

(8) The present situation is not without analogy. While former democracies are maintained by force in the Eastern heartland, a constant pressure is placed upon Western democracies for the purpose of neutralizing them and having them enter, if possible, into the sphere of influence of Marxist-Leninist ideology. Convinced that it contains the secret for the total liberation of all men and all peoples, this ideology considers itself authorized to impose on all what it believes to be in their best interest. Our purpose is not to foster a Manichean conception of the world: all the evil on one side and all the good on the other! The West is itself also sick. Materialism—whether theoretical as in the East or practical as in the

---

[4] *The Church in the Modern World*, no. 80, 2.

West—is a deadly illness for humanity, and the Marxist-Leninist states do not have the monopoly on imperialism. They sometimes even make disciples in systems which are directly opposed to them. But it would be unfair to put everyone into the same category and close our eyes to the aggressive and dominating character of Marxist-Leninist ideology. In this ideology, everything, even the aspirations of nations for peace, must be utilized for the conquest of the world.

(9) Under these conditions, does not the absolute condemnation of all war place peace-loving peoples at the mercy of those who are motivated by an ideology of domination? In order to escape war, these people risk succumbing to other forms of violence and injustice: colonization, alienation, privation of their liberty and their identity. When played out to the end, peace at any price leads a nation to every kind of capitulation. A unilateral disarmament can even provoke the aggression of one's neighbors by feeding the temptation to seize a prey which is all too ready for the taking: "After all, it would be much better for us to become their captives. We would be slaves, undoubtedly, but we would be alive", declare the fellow countrymen of Judith, terrorized by the extortions of Holofernes— which their defeatism encouraged (Judith 7:27). In a world where one man still preys upon another, to change oneself into a lamb could be to provoke the wolf. Less enlightened acts of generosity have sometimes provoked the very evils that they were believed to be capable of eliminating. A poorly adapted nonviolence can unleash a series of chain reactions of inexplicable violence. This is why the German bishops wrote: "A unilateral renunciation of this protection and resistance may be understood as weakness and possibly as an invitation to perpetrate political blackmail. In fact, such a renunciation may foster the very things it is designed to prevent, namely, the oppression of the innocent and the infliction of suffering and brutality on them."[5] Patriotism is a virtue. It should not be confused with an exaggerated sense of nationalism or blind xenophobia. It includes a country's legitimate concern to preserve its self-identity and defend itself against an unjust aggression.

[5] "La Justice construit la paix", pastoral letter of the bishops of West Germany, French trans. in *La Documentation catholique* (1983), 582; English trans. above, "Out of Justice, Peace", no. 104.

The Non-Violent Alternative

(10) More and more people are saying that we are not limited to the simple alternative of war or surrender. We are not caught in this dilemma; there is a way out, a "narrow way", like that of the kingdom (Mt 7:13). But it is one which is practical: nonviolence. The non-violent currents are multiple, from absolute nonviolence on all fronts to non-violent resistance: concerned with taking into account the reality of the threat and of the aggressiveness in the world, this latter current refuses surrender and peace at any price.[6] Christians find here a resonance with the gospel.

(11) These have understood the counsel "not to resist evildoers" and even to "turn the other cheek" (Mt 5:30). After having invited Peter to return his sword to its scabbard, Christ was silent before his judges (Mt 26.63, 27.14) and went forth "as a sheep to the slaughter, a lamb who would not open his mouth" (Is 53:7). He will remind men until the end of time that the last word cannot be violence.

(12) The nonresistance of Christ, the pardon that he offers, is the salt which alone can save the world from the corruption of violence. Non violence remains a summons to each man and even to human communities. But can nonviolence be a policy for states? The Church has always recognized the right that political powers have to respond to violence by means of force. Christ did not contest the authority of Pilate (Jn 19:11). And Saint Paul recognized the law of the sword—in the case of Nero! (Cf Rom 13:1–5; 1 Pet 2:13–14). Nonviolence is a risk which individuals can take. Can states, whose function is to defend peace, take this risk?

(13) In the world of violence and of injustice, which is our own, politicians have the right to safeguard the common good of the state over which they exercise a responsibility. Peace is a constituent of this common good, but so also, inseparably, are justice, solidarity and liberty. In order to achieve this, they must have the means to discourage, as much as possible, an eventual aggressor. The state has the monopoly of force over its own territory.[7] It is better to demonstrate this monopoly rather than to have to exercise it. In cases of necessity, however, the state can have recourse to it: A just and measured recourse still is at the service of peace and the common good, for it dissuades citizens from taking justice into

---

[6] One can find a recent consideration under a significant title: De J. Toulat, *Combattants de la nonviolence* (Paris: Cerf, 1983). Cf. idem, *Un Combat pour la vie* (Nouvelle Cité, 1982), chap. 7: "La Bombe ou la vie".

[7] Cf. J. Freund, *Qu'est-ce que la politique?* (Paris: Seuil, 1965), 118, 131, 167.

their own hands. We know in fact what injustices and what disorders ensue when a state of law gives way to the law of the strongest. Bands of vigilantes, intent upon self-defense, represent a political regression in the juridical organization of the state. The threat of "public" force and, in cases of necessity, its use in conformity with law are a political step forward, progress: A "policed" state—which is not a police state—is a guarantee of peace for its citizens.

(14) In international relations, unfortunately, no authority is yet powerful enough and sufficiently workable to impose this state of law. We cannot deny each country the right to legitimate defense against external threats as well as internal dangers.[8] We cannot deny it the right to acquire for itself the means which are adapted to the threats which it must face, and this sufficiently in advance, for a proper defense cannot be set in motion only at the onset of international crises.

(15) However, do not the partisans of non-violent resistance correctly say that the most effective defense would be passive resistance to those occupying one's country? Some techniques of non-violent action have given evidence of this. Gandhi is especially cited in this particular regard. All of this must be taken into consideration. But can we declare that these methods are effective to the point of rendering superfluous the necessity of an armed defense? One can well imagine what slaughters would be produced by resistance and even a passive resistance among entire peoples who are without external military supports and are handed over to less scrupulous tormentors.[9] However, the logic (threat, counter-threat) cannot last forever. We will see this later on. Are the nonviolent correct in the long run? In the immediate and proximate future, however, the nonviolent alternative still appears very hazardous. In any case, it is not sufficiently clear to justify reproaching those responsible for the life and integrity of the nation for having recourse to a deterrence of armed counter-threat.

---

[8] Cf. *The Church in the Modern World*, nos. 79, 4 and 82, 2.

[9] It could be asked, for example, what would have happened if Gandhi, in place of having as a partner Lord Louis Mountbatten, had had one of the celebrated tormentors of Europe. The persecution of non-violent people in the East should also give us pause for reflection about any movement down a one-way street.

2. NUCLEAR DETERRENCE

(16) Nuclear capacity confers on the states which have acquired it an unquestionable power. Without pretending to have parity with the superpowers, a lesser power has presently the means of inflicting on an aggressor much more powerful than itself intolerable damage. We have heard this matter referred to as the "equalizing power of the atom". Certainly, a relative equality! But, our strategists tell us, the systems of nuclear arms allow us to inflict upon an aggressor damages disproportionate to the advantages that he would expect to gain from his aggression. This is "the deterrent of the strong by the weak", in the words of our experts.

Some New Questions

(17) We will not enter into the technical debates of specialists regarding the credibility of our defense, regarding the deployment of our classical, nuclear, tactical and strategic means and their relationship to and compatibility with other systems of those involved in a common alliance. Each poses specific ethical problems which call for the virtue of prudence: the morality of an effective retaliation by conventional arms, first use of a tactical nuclear strike (only in principle), response by a second strike, and so forth. Other problems arise with respect to articulation of the relationship with one's allies, the control of action by political power and up to what point, and so forth. In these very technical problems, which have an ethical dimension, we must guard against two extremes:
1) To renounce any ethical judgment as if one were going to leave these matters, so fraught with human significance, solely to a technical logic.
2) Peremptory judgments of the deductive type which would make light of the complex technical problems involved.

(18) Between these two extremes, it is appropriate to formulate a prudential judgment which adheres closely to the contingencies that have been weighed with great circumspection and which recognizes the interplay of certitudes and questions: A respect for the nature of what is at stake and for the value of responsible statements is required here.[10]

---

[10] Aristotle reminds us "that we should not look for the same degree of certainty in all matters, but in each to the extent that the subject allows"; and St. Thomas comments: "Now

(19) But here we would like to dwell on global perspectives.[11]

(20) The central question which is being asked, then, is the following: In the present geopolitical context, can a country which is being threatened in its life, liberty or identity morally have the right to oppose this radical threat with an effective counter-threat, even one which is nuclear?

(21) Up until now, while stressing the limited character of such a stance and the enormous risk which it entails, the Catholic Church has not believed it necessary to condemn it. As the Second Vatican Council states:

> Undoubtedly, armaments are not amassed merely for use in wartime. Since the defensive strength of any nation is thought to depend on its capacity for immediate retaliation, the stockpiling of arms which grows from year to year serves, in a way hitherto unthought of, as a deterrent to potential attackers. Many people look upon this as the most effective way known at the present time for maintaining some sort of peace among nations.
>
> Whatever one may think of this form of deterrent, people are convinced that the arms race, which quite a few countries have entered, is no infallible way of maintaining real peace and that the resulting so-called balance of power is no sure way and genuine path to achieving it.[12]

(22) In this instance it is a matter of a momentary or temporary response, in order to react to a limited situation from which a way out must be found as soon as possible, so great is the risk.

> Warned by the possibility of the catastrophes that man has created, let us profit by the respite we now enjoy, thanks to the divine favor, to take stock of our responsibilities and find ways of resolving controversies in a manner worthy of human beings.[13]

---

because the subject matter of prudence is composed of contingent individual incidents, which form the setting for human acts, the certitude of prudence is not such as to remove all uneasiness of mind (*sollicitudo*)" (*Summa Theologica*, IIa IIae, q. 47, art. 9, ad 2). [Practical or moral certitude is not to be resolved into the theoretical certitude of a theological or legal scheme: This is a central point in St. Thomas' thought which he develops from Aristotle.—Tr.]

It is clear that the formulation of an ethical judgment can only be done by means of a gradual gathering together of the facts by means of a multidisciplinary discussion among the interested parties (cf. *The Church in the Modern World*, no. 33, 2) and by framing its expression in accordance with the degrees of certitude acquired.

[11] Regarding these debates see, for example, Gen. L. Poirier, "Essais de strategie theorique", in *Documentation française* (1982), and Fr. de Rose, *Contre la strategie de Curiaces* (Paris: Julliard, 1983).

[12] *The Church in the Modern World*, no. 81, 1 and 2.

[13] Ibid., no. 81, 4.

(23) Time marches on, the time allotted diminishes, and the American Bishops have issued a cry of alarm to the world: "The Challenge of Peace".[14] However, the situation has not so deteriorated that this practical judgment of the Council has been rendered superfluous. Pope John Paul II himself wrote last year:

> Under present conditions, deterrence based on equilibrium—certainly not as an end in itself, but as a stage on the way to progressive disarmament—can still be judged to be morally acceptable. However, to insure peace it is indispensable not to be content with a minimum which is always fraught with a real danger of explosion.[15]

(24) If the Church speaks in this way, it is not without serious reasons. Only a defensive posture allows for the legitimation of this mortal game being played out at the gates of Hell: "One cannot love with offensive weapons in one's hands", Paul VI stated at the United Nations in 1965.[16]

(25) "Offensive weapons!" A sad expression, an almost useless qualification which says a great deal about our distressed situation. The Pope knew well that offensive weapons and defensive weapons are, by and large, the same and that the offensive nature of these weapons is to be found in the heart of man. That is why the Pope continued: "As long as man remains the weak, changeable, and even wicked being that he often shows himself to be, defensive arms will, alas, be necessary." And the Pope who expresses himself in this way is the very one who at the same time stated, "Never again one against the other, never, never again." "Humanity will have to put an end to war or it is war which will put an end to humanity" (as John F. Kennedy stated). "Never again war, war never again!"[17]

Threat Is Not Use

(26) This logic is, to be sure, a logic of distress: It cannot hide or conceal its congenital weakness. Certainly, it is in order not to wage war that nations seek to show themselves capable of waging it. Peace is still being served when the aggressor is discouraged and constrained to the beginning of wisdom as a result of an appropriate fear. The threat of force is not

[14] French ed. published in *La Documentation catholique* (July 24, 1983), 715–62.

[15] "Message à l'ONU, June 1982", in *La Documentation catholique* (July 4, 1982), 666.

[16] Reference omitted in French original. [Ed.]

[17] *Discours au Concile* (Paris: Centurion, 1966), 329 and 327–28; *La Documentation catholique* (1965), cols. 1734–35.

the use of force. It is the basis of deterrence, and this is often forgotten when the same moral qualification is attributed to the threat as to the use of force.

(27) Nevertheless, the danger of the logic of deterrence is immediately evident. In order not to allow a possible aggressor to have illusions about the credibility of our defenses, we must show ourselves ready to use our weapons if deterrence should fail.

(28) But the moral legitimacy of this move from possession to use is more than problematical. This is all the more true in France because our deterrence is a "deterrence of the strong by the weak", a poor man's deterrence: Because of the lack of diversified means of deterrence, our deterrence still rests on an anti-city strategy, itself clearly condemned, without appeal, by the Council: "Every act of war directed to the indiscriminate destruction of whole cities or vast areas with their in-habitants is a crime against God and man, which merits firm and unequi-vocal condemnation."[18]

(29) But threat is not use. Does the immorality of use render the threat immoral? This is not evident. For, as the Council says,[19] "they cannot ignore the complexity of the situation as it stands." In the situation of violence and sin which is that of the world in which we live, politicians and military personnel have a duty in justice to refuse to give in to the nuclear blackmail to which the nation would be subjected. "Charity is not a substitute for law", the German Bishops wrote. "Love even requires, first and foremost, the observance of human rights as the basic rights of every society. Acknowledgment of these rights forms the bridge to peace and freedom, both internally and externally."[20]

(30) Faced with a choice between two evils, both of them all but unavoidable, capitulations or counter-threats, one chooses the lesser with-out pretending that one is choosing a moral good.[21] It is clear what

---

[18] *The Church in the Modern World*, no. 80, 4.

[19] Ibid., no. 82, 2.

[20] "La Justice construit la paix", *La Documentation catholique* (1983), 583; "Out of Justice, Peace", above, no. 113.

[21] As early as the Council, the Archbishop of Liverpool, Archbishop Beck, had attempted to deal with this difficult problem: "It would seem to be evident that a government possessing a deterrent of nuclear arms, which threatens to make use of them, finds itself in a near occasion of grave sin. One could respond that we do not have effective international institutions to maintain peace, that is to say, so long as a country cannot really give up its deterrent without grave risks for its own liberty as well as its cultural and spiritual values, that near occasion of sin is what moralists call a 'necessary occasion'. It is necessary to accept this occasion as a compromise so long as there cannot be created a balance of confidence and

recourse to nuclear deterrence supposes, if it is to be morally acceptable: that it applies only to defense; that overarming be avoided—deterrence is reached at the moment when the formulated threat renders unreasonable the aggression of a third party; that all precautions be taken to avoid a "mistake" or the intervention of a madman, or of a terrorist, and so on; that the nation which takes the risk of nuclear deterrence likewise pursue a constructive policy in favor of peace.

A Deadly Spiral

(31) Actually, our situation, in itself so perilous, is aggravated even more by the unstable nature of the balance which has been acquired. Despite all the precautions that have been taken, the world is not safe from an accidental outbreak of war and this becomes more possible the more countries there are that engage in this deadly game. Moreover, the obsession with a technical breakthrough on the part of one of these players in the game—a discovery, an important development which temporarily guarantees him an unquestionable superiority, thereby tempting him to provoke a test of strength—all of this fuels the spiral of the arms race.[22] It is an exhausting race for the protagonists, but also for the others who, in one way or another, finance the overarming of the great powers. These fruitless expenditures impoverish the poor if only by hindering them from sharing in the resources that are devoted to armament. And the growing disparity between the north and the south increases the tensions that can engender conflict by "calling down upon them the judgment of

discussion which ought to replace the present balance of terror. We must remind nations of the grave obligation which they have, at the present time, of rendering remote this occasion of sin and showing themselves prepared to accept limitations on their normal sovereignty in the measure necessary to create an effective international authority" (*La Documentation catholique* [1965], col. 2088).

A proximate occasion of serious sin! But a necessary occasion, as classical moral theologians say. Once more we are up against an ethic of distress, acceptable only on the condition that it operate from a dynamic perspective of gradualness, of seeking to go beyond the status quo, and that under no circumstances there be any pretense of making a good out of a lesser evil!

[22] "It cannot be denied that the material fact of a country continuing to develop its capacity for nuclear response, even if this development is tied to a wish to avoid war, involves in itself a kind of temptation, the temptation of resorting to nuclear threats. This is one of the weaknesses of this position and one cannot insure oneself against it except by confiding the conduct of the affairs of the nation to men who are deeply conscious of their responsibility. A 'nuclear nation' must be a reasonable nation, resolutely directed toward peace, but not peace at any price."

God and the wrath of the poor, with consequences no one can foretell" (as Paul VI mentioned in his encyclical *Populorum progressio*).[23]

(32) "All public and private squandering of wealth, all expenditure prompted by motives of national or personal ostentation, every exhausting armaments race, becomes an intolerable scandal", as he also said.[24]

(33) Nuclear deterrence has not prevented some atrocious wars since 1945. One hundred and thirty conflicts which have taken between 30 and 50 million lives have been counted. But it has staved off the direct suicidal confrontation between the superpowers. It cannot be denied that deterrence has played a certain regulatory role; it serves as a fundamental but nonetheless dangerous wisdom, for if fear can be the beginning of wisdom, it is not wisdom itself. And "non-war" based upon fear is not peace. This fear, left to itself, can be doubly deadly, either because it diminishes as we grow used to it or, on the contrary, because it produces among some an overpowering fascination.

3. ESTABLISHING PEACE

(34) "He who lives by the sword will perish by the sword" (Mt 26:52). Certainly, in this instance also, extending this to cover the defense of a whole nation forbids us to resort to improper oversimplification. But a clear direction is indicated.

The Non-Violent Reference

(35) The Church does not encourage exaggerated pacifism. She has never preached unilateral disarmament, knowing full well that this could be a signal for violence on the part of an aggressive military, political and ideological complex. But she recognizes the message of the Gospel in its call to nonviolence: This is a prophetic call regarding the destructive nature of violence. "Anger of any kind, even justified, contorts your face", runs an old Polish proverb. Even when legitimate, violence can be dreadful. This is so to the greatest extent when it is a matter of the suicidal spiral which we have just mentioned. This introduces the world into a situation of sin and each of us into networks of responsibility in which our conscience is involved. Moreover, the constant appeals of men and

[23] *Populorum progressio*, no. 49.
[24] Ibid., no. 53.

women who, looking beyond the present sad necessity, invite us to reject the logic of death, must be heard.

(36) Has not the time come, without of course giving up the right of armed defense, to examine carefully the role and effectiveness of non-violent techniques and to evaluate the risks and possibilities of these non-violent techniques as carefully as we have examined the risks of the arms race?

(37) In the very heart of the city, those who are most sensitive to the risk of violence once unleashed ought to be heard. They serve the common good by preventing the logic of the short term from closing its infernal circle. Rightly, they refuse to be considered idealists. It is realistic to call forth the possibility for transformation which can be found residing in the reality of today—perhaps they are pioneers of the future.

(38) Nonviolence "should not be defined as merely the refusal of violence. It cannot be reduced to techniques employed by Gandhi who did not, moreover, make an absolute out of it. Nonviolence is a mentality which draws all its strength from the beatitudes. According to the expression of Olivier Lacombe, 'Gandhi forced Christians to remember that the gospel can work.' The nonviolent are engaged in bearing witness in the midst of men who are otherwise resigned to an ever-present state of violence".[25] Such a vocation can neither be accepted lightly nor treated lightly.

(39) But when it pleads for the reality of tomorrow, nonviolence cannot ignore the real gravity of today. It is important that men of courage also assume its worries and constraints.

Disarmament, a Common Task

(40) At the same time that it recognizes this present necessity of armed defense, the Church urges constantly to go beyond it. "It is our clear duty to spare no effort in order to work for the moment when all war will be completely outlawed by international agreement. This goal, of course, requires the establishment of a universally acknowledged public authority vested with the effective power to ensure security for all, regard for justice and respect for law", the Council stated.[26]

(41) The line that has been drawn is clear: On the one hand, it is necessary to reinforce international organizations even if in this domain

---

[25] Cardinal Etchegaray, "*L'Eglise aujourd'hui à Marseille*".

[26] *The Church in the Modern World*, no. 82, 1.

things have made little progress—which led John Paul II to specify further:

> Obviously the object of international dialogue will also concern itself with the dangerous arms race in such a way as to progressively reduce it, as I suggested in the message I sent to the United Nations last June, and in conformity with the message which the learned members of the Pontifical Academy of Sciences took on my behalf to the leaders of the nuclear powers. Instead of being at the service of people, the economy is becoming militarized. Development and well-being are subordinated to security. Science and technology are being degraded into the auxiliaries of war. The Holy See will not grow weary of insisting upon the need to slow down the arms race through progressive negotiations, calling for reciprocity. The Holy See will continue to encourage all steps, even the smallest ones, of reasonable dialogue in this very important sphere.[27]

(42) As always the Pope speaks of progressive and reciprocal disarmament. These efforts towards disarmament are incumbent not only on a few leaders and experts. All citizens are involved, first of all by virtue of their being "taxpayers"—and then as potential victims! This is why they must also be "advisors", provided they resolutely seek the serious information demanded by the seriousness of what is at stake, namely, the peace and the freedom of the nation and the world: "Nevertheless, men should take heed not to entrust themselves only to the efforts of others, while remaining careless about their own attitudes. For government officials, who must simultaneously guarantee the good of their own people and promote the universal good, depend very much on public opinion and feeling", as Vatican II also observed.[28]

The Necessary But Difficult Dialogue

(43) This progress supposes a permanent desire for dialogue. The Holy Father devoted his message for the World Day of Peace of January 1, 1983, to this vital necessity. He stressed the fruitfulness of dialogue in all relationships. With his characteristic realism he confronted head-on that type of dialogue which is apparently made impossible, when human perversity reduces it to a monologue:

[27] Message for the World Day of Peace 1983, in *La Documentation catholique* (Jan. 16, 1983), 70.
[28] Ibid., no. 82, 3.

This attitude can conceal quite simply the blind and deaf selfishness of the people, or more often the will to power of its leaders. It also happens that this attitude coincides with an exaggerated and out-of-date concept of the sovereignty and security of the state. The state then runs the risk of becoming the object of worship which is, so to speak, unquestionable. It runs the risk of justifying the most questionable undertakings. . . .

Finally, when certain parties are nurtured by ideologies which, in spite of their declarations, are opposed to the dignity of the human person, to just aspirations according to the healthy principles of reason, of the natural and eternal law (cf. *Pacem in Terris, A.A.S.* 55 [1963], 300), by ideologies which see in struggle the moving force of history, which see in force the source of rights, which see in the detection of the enemy the ABC of politics, dialogue is stiff and sterile. Or, if it still exists, it is, in reality, superficial and falsified. It becomes very difficult, not to say impossible. There follows an almost complete lack of communication between countries and blocs. Even international institutions are paralyzed. The failure of dialogue then runs the risk of serving the arms race.

However, even in what can be considered as an impasse to the extent that individuals support such ideologies, the attempt to have a lucid dialogue still seems necessary in order to clear away obstacles and to work for the possible establishment of peace on particular points. This is to be done by counting on common sense, on the possibilities of danger for everyone and on the just aspirations which the people themselves in large part hold dear.[29]

(44) The Church is aware of the limits of dialogue and even of its ambiguity. However, she continually calls for it and positively encourages it by participating herself in international meetings such as those at Helsinki and at Belgrade, for example. The Church merely wants everyone to understand both what is at stake and what the limits of dialogue are. Some are tempted to be ironical about this ambiguous dialogue. But if we admit the possibility of a deterrent "of distress" for a situation of distress, must we not also admit a dialogue of distress? With regard to the dialogue of the deaf, which is what our current threats and counter-threats amount to, would not a dialogue of the hard-of-hearing be a sign of progress? To talk, to listen, to try to understand the language of one's neighbor, is that not already a form of mutual understanding aimed at reversing the upward spiral of Babel?

(45) For we cannot remain in the present stalemate: Non-war is not

[29] *La Documentation catholique* (1983), 69.

peace. It is a necessary but inadequate condition of it. "Non-war" that is not accompanied by a constructive effort to establish a real peace is of necessity provisional. The urgent necessity for getting beyond war and its threat places man in the position of having to construct or build peace. The radical nature of nuclear conflict henceforth must disabuse anyone of the pretension of being able to win a nuclear war. Deterrence appears as a solution of distress, eminently provisional. There is therefore no alternative for us: We must win the peace.

Winning the Peace

(46) Clearly this is going to involve long and exacting labor, for it requires a real conversion of hearts. A lasting peace, beyond mere co-existence, demands a certain agreement, a harmony between persons, human communities and nations. It demands institutions for meeting, dialogue and the building of a better world—if we are not to remain on the level of good intentions. But these good intentions would only be deceptive Towers of Babel if they are not the incarnation of spiritual attitudes which John XXIII articulated around four principles: truth, justice, solidarity and liberty.

(47) There is no peace without truth. Lies, recriminations and mis-information fuel mistrust. Without a minimum of trust, without respect for the word which one gives, there is no longer any common life possible. This is normally learned within the bosom of the family, based on marriage, a place in which one's word is given and held to. This commitment, this conjugal covenant, is, more than one thinks, the basis for all truly human social life.

(48) There is no peace without liberty. A genuine person aspires to take his own destiny into his own hands. One of the precious acquisitions of democracy is precisely the establishment of a social, economic and political sphere which allows for the participation of all in that which touches upon the life of all. That is why wherever the legitimate liberty of persons and of human groups is scorned, there is no real peace. A power can impose itself by force, but this power is not an "authority"; it is endured, but it is not recognized, and at the earliest opportunity the slaves revolt.

(49) There is no peace without justice. Injustices in the distribution of goods and in the status of persons engender irreparable conflicts. Without the proper distribution of the fruits of common effort, citizens are unable to identify themselves with the nation and will not be motivated to defend what they think to be the privilege of those who have these possessions.

But even more than respect for goods, for *having*, justice demands respect for *being*, for the dignity and the basic equality of persons. When entire groups of citizens encamp at the gates of the city, they have no inclination to defend it. If the city does not recognize them as its own, they in their turn will refuse to recognize it as their own common good. Internal peace becomes fragile when this cohesion is lacking. And in the community of nations a frustrated country becomes aggressive and engenders conflicts. The Bible recalls this to us: "Peace is the fruit of justice" (Is 32:17).

(50) Nor can there be any real peace without solidarity. Beyond simple justice, charity demands that the human community know how to organize itself in order to promote a real common good. In the past many people were not aware of this. But today the mass media weave a close-knit network of communications. If, in parallel fashion, a network of exchanges and solidarity is not established, the human community is likely to explode in the collisions between the economic underdevelopment of the southern hemisphere and the moral underdevelopment of the northern hemisphere. For, as Paul VI stated: "Both for nations and for individual men, avarice is the most evident form of moral underdevelopment."[30]

(51) Naturally, these fundamental values which inspire a genuine peace must take form in suitable institutions. It is important to restate here what the Council and the encyclicals *Pacem in terris* and *Populorum progressio* said about the building up of the international community. This cannot be realized without learning new modes of international conduct:

> Already existing international and regional organizations certainly deserve well of the human race. They represent the first attempts at laying the foundations on an international level for a community of all men to work towards the solutions of the very serious problems of our times, and specifically towards the encouragement of progress everywhere and the prevention of wars of all kinds.[31]

(52) Finally, there is no genuine peace without true respect for the rights of man. "Peace among peoples and in the community of nations itself is based above all on justice, that is to say, on the effective recognition of the fundamental rights of all countries and of all citizens", Pope John Paul II recently wrote.[32]

[30] *Populorum progressio*, no. 19.
[31] *The Church in the Modern World*, no. 84, 3; cf. no. 85, 3.
[32] Letter to Msgr. Manfredini for the anniversary of *Pacem in terris* and *Populorum progressio*, in *La Documentation catholique* (1983), 551.

(53) The mention of the rights of man, in a very singular fashion, enlarges our horizons. This takes us well beyond "non-war"and even beyond the just distribution of goods within nations and between nations themselves. It is man himself about whom we are concerned.

(54) This leads us toward a conception of peace which goes far beyond simply social perspectives. The peace about which the Bible speaks is situated on another level. Integral peace is the harmony of man with himself, with the world, with others, and with God. Can this genuine peace reign in this world of ours? Like total nonviolence, it can only attain to that degree of fullness in the heart of saints such as Francis of Assisi, for example. But these witnesses call all men to prepare for the return of the Prince of Peace (Is 9:5) who alone will be able to establish total justice. In order to hasten his coming, they appeal to us to construct, in our turn, a world which will already be inspired by the beatitudes: "Happy are the peacemakers, for they will be called sons of God" (Mt 5:9).

(55) Situating the peace on this level is tantamount to heightening the debate. This is incontestable. But it is normal. A people cannot live for a long time with its eyes riveted upon the radar screens of its territorial surveillance or upon the statistical charts of its economists. All this is important but remains in the order of means. Beyond the means of living arises the question of the reasons for living: for persons, but also for nations and for the entire human race. And this is a question of culture— that is to say, a spiritual question.

(56) In this regard, have we not, for several decades in our country, been in the process of cutting ourselves off rather dangerously from our deepest roots?

(57) When justice and solidarity are forgotten, when foreigners and immigrants see themselves being reproached for filling the cradles and the kindergarten classes which we are leaving empty, when "love is without life and life without love",[33] when family life is in ruins, when factions and groups hurl condemnations at one another, when the faith is systematically ridiculed, the absolute becomes relative and the relative absolute. Thus the underlying inspiration of a nation is lost and the entire country doubts its identity and its vocation.

[33] Cardinal Lustiger at Bonn, in *La Documentation catholique* (1981), 982.

(58) When Pope John Paul asked of us at Paris: "France, eldest daughter of the Church, are you being faithful to the promises of your Baptism?"—was this question, indeed, out of place? Even before this, Father G. Fessard alerted us: "France, take care lest you lose your soul!"[34]

(59) Is not this question also being addressed to the West and to the countries of the East? Is not the major threat for France and for Europe spiritual? With what force is the practical Western materialism going to be able to counter, in the long run, its cousin, the theoretical materialism of the East? Do not both the East and the West have to return to their roots which are spiritual, as Maurice Clavel and Solzhenitsyn and many others are recalling to us? The situation of sin in which we find ourselves is summoning all of us to conversion: "But unless you are converted, you shall all perish" (Lk 13:3).

(60) Men of good will know in the depths of their hearts that a human community is not a society with limited responsibility; it is not a clan held together by a common danger; it is not merely a family held together by a simple bond of blood. A human community needs to have a soul. But how will men be able to recognize each other as brothers if they refuse to recognize a common Father?

(61) In any case, we Christians are convinced of this. Conscious of "the wall of hatred" which separates men (Eph 2:14), knowing full well that it arose from the very dawn of time, cemented by jealousy, violence, and revenge (cf. Gen 4:1–8), we are well aware of the foolish desire of God. He wishes to snatch men from the law of the jungle in order to make them a people of sons, a people of brothers. It is an impossible task. But "what is impossible for men is possible for God" (Lk 18:27). He has sent his Son in order to gather into one the children of God who are scattered abroad (Jn 11:52). "In his flesh he has destroyed the wall of separation and hatred. . . . He has thereby wished to create in him one single new man, thereby establishing peace and reconciling them with God" (Eph 2:14–16).

(62) In this same Spirit, we desire to continue his work by confiding it in prayer to our common Father. Without denying the present state of distress, we wish to go beyond it, with respect for various vocations within the city of man, when they proceed from an enlightened and effective love for peace.

(63) In a particularly difficult situation for men of our age, we have wished, in our function as pastors, to shed some light "by joining the light

---

[34] G. Fessard, *Cahier du Temoignage chretien* (1942).

of Revelation to the experience of all",[35] in order to mark out the road to peace.

(64) Many points remain to be clarified, many trails remain to be explored, many fields remain open where legitimate differences can and must confront each other. An honest dialogue is a way to peace; it can open itself to pardon and reconciliation.

(65) Various groups are available to Christians for the purpose of common research, for conversion of mind and heart, and for knowledge about issues. The seriousness of the debate actually calls for genuine information. Taking different approaches, such movements or organizations as Pax Christi or Justice and Peace, which have a vocation in the Church, can be utilized effectively. But this effort is not reserved only to some. Peace is the business of everyone. The World Day of Peace invites each person to take at least some small steps at his own pace. It moves us all to reflection, prayer and exchange.

(66) Final peace is only to be found with God, beyond death. It is received as a gratuitous gift. But it is prepared for during this life: "Happy are the peacemakers, for they will be called the sons of God" (Mt 5:10). "Peace on earth" (Lk 2:14) bears the seed of the peace of heaven. It is perhaps a grace that men and women of our age are in the process of discovering in the midst of the present distress: "Against each other", we will never again win the war. "With each other",[36] we can win the peace!

Lourdes, November 8, 1983

---

[35] *The Church in the Modern World*, no. 33, 2.
[36] Cf. Paul VI at the United Nations in 1965.

APPENDIX
TOWARDS A NUCLEAR MORALITY

A LETTER BY BASIL CARDINAL HUME,
PRIMATE OF ENGLAND

(1) Throughout October I attended the International Synod of Bishops in Rome which brought together bishops from every part of the world to explore the question of how to make peace with God and with other people in today's world. The Synod deplored and condemned "warlike aggressiveness, violence and terrorism; the building up of arsenals of both conventional, and especially nuclear arms, and the scandalous trade in all weapons of war".

(2) The sense of anxiety felt by the Synod in the face of these terrors was reflected by Pope John Paul II, who declared himself "very troubled" at the tense international situation and sent urgent messages to the Russian and American leaders.

(3) On returning to London I found new undercurrents of anxiety and disquiet caused by the impending arrival of cruise and Pershing missiles. In recent days the debate about nuclear armaments and possible nuclear conflict has been brought home to people much more sharply than before. It is not an easy task to see clearly the way forward and to come to terms with these complex and threatening issues.

(4) Tension has undoubtedly increased because of the public protests and mass demonstrations of the recent past. In a free society, the peace movements play an important role. They bring before us the terrible questions we might otherwise ignore but which must be answered. They rightly alert us to the dangers of nuclear escalation and proliferation. They compel us to question whether new weapons are intended to deter or whether they serve an aggressive purpose.

(5) Inevitably, though, the peace movements bring pressure to bear primarily on the governments of the West and not on those of the

East. In communist regimes movements critical of official policy are rarely tolerated. There are different perceptions in East and West about the threat to peace.

(6) No one can deny the moral dilemma which faces us today. On the one hand we have a grave obligation to prevent nuclear war from ever occurring. On the other hand, the state has the right and duty of legitimate self-defense, thus ensuring for its citizens justice, freedom and independence. Although nothing could ever justify the use of nuclear arms as weapons of massive and indiscriminate slaughter, yet to abandon them without adequate safeguards may help to destabilize the existing situation and may dramatically increase the risk of nuclear blackmail.

(7) There is a tension, then, between the moral imperative not to use such inhuman weapons and a policy of nuclear deterrence with its declared willingness to use them if attacked. To condemn all use and yet to accept deterrence places us in a seemingly contradictory position.

(8) It is then perhaps surprising, and puzzling to some Christians, that Pope John Paul II could say to the United Nations on June 11, 1982: "In current conditions 'deterrence' based on balance, certainly not as an end in itself, but as a stage on the way towards a progressive disarmament, can still be judged morally acceptable. Nonetheless, in order to preserve peace, it is indispensable not to be satisfied with this minimum which is always susceptible to the real danger of explosion".

(9) It is noteworthy that every Catholic bishops' conference pronouncing subsequently on these issues has followed this judgment. As an authoritative pronouncement of the Holy Father, it is an important contribution to Catholic thinking.

(10) In the first place, this view recognizes that, because of the world situation, deterrence may be accepted as the lesser of two evils, without in any way regarding it as good in itself. Furthermore, this view can be held even by those who reject the morality of nuclear deterrence. It constitutes an acknowledgment that even a morally flawed defense policy cannot simply be dismantled immediately and without reference to the response of potential enemies.

(11) To retain moral credibility, however, there must be a firm and effective intention to extricate ourselves from the present fearful situation as quickly as possible. We must work towards our declared objective of deescalation and disarmament. But mutual and verifiable disarmament can be achieved only in stages, and so gradually. This approach is both realistic and morally acceptable.

(12) The acceptance of deterrence on strict conditions and as a tem-

porary expedient leading to progressive disarmament is emerging as the most widely accepted view of the Roman Catholic Church.

(13) It may in some respects be an untidy view, risky and provisional, yet it is at the same time important. It has immediate consequences.

(14) First, the Church hereby gives a strictly qualified assent to the policy of deterrence but solely on condition that it constitutes a stage towards disarmament. This is a crucial condition. If any government, in the East or West, does not take steps to reduce its nuclear weapons and limit their deployment, it must expect its citizens in increasing numbers to be doubtful of its sincerity and alienated from its defense policies.

(15) Second, it would be wrong to apply to the policy of nuclear deterrence the same moral condemnation that would be given to the actual use of nuclear weapons against civilian targets.

(16) Third, since the purpose and intention of deterrence is to avoid war and keep the peace, service personnel can be rightly commended as custodians of the security and freedom of their fellow countrymen and as contributors to the maintenance of peace. Nonetheless they, too, face grave moral issues which they themselves do not ignore.

(17) Fourth, deterrence has to be seen clearly as a means of preventing war and not of waging it. If it fails and the missiles are launched, then we shall have moved into a new situation. And those concerned will have to bear a heavy responsibility.

(18) Disarmament is hindered by mutual fear and hostility between the superpowers. They already have the capacity to destroy each other many times over. There is urgent need to halt the spiral of armaments. Our vast expenditure on national defense is out of balance and should be cut back. It necessarily diverts resources from other needs, both those of the Third World and our own at home. People everywhere have a right to know in what ways their governments are pursuing policies that will lead to disarmament. Without such policies, deterrence has to be condemned.

(19) We are all faced with an agonizing and unclear situation, further complicated by state secrecy on security matters. Christians must themselves recognize that there is room for differences of opinion in the present situation. All of us must retain the right to our conscientious beliefs. And I would judge that this does not give us the right seriously to defy the law in the present situation. We must have due regard for democratic processes and for the institutions of a free society.

(20) Within the framework of our democratic system, the Christian can find scope enough to work with wholehearted enthusiasm and commitment for the cause of peace and for the making of a world where both sides

in our present confrontation will be encouraged to enter with greater determination the path of negotiation and effective disarmament.

(21) It seems to me that we often approach the problem from the wrong angle. Our representatives have spent many hours of negotiation over the contents of successive disarmament proposals. But disarmament will follow the lowering of tension and the building of confidence and not vice versa. We have to stress rather the need for political will on both sides to achieve "detente".

(22) It is possible, if leaders and people want it, to overcome fears and insecurity in international relationships. History abounds in examples. If the confidence to live and let live is built up on both sides, then it should not prove impossible to reflect a newly found security by means of progressive disarmament proposals. Here is a task for all of us, but especially for our political parties and leaders.

(23) The present situation is grave. Those with political power must have the will to discover a better way to achieve peace than through amassing nuclear weapons. The future of humanity depends on it.

DATE DUE

JE 21 93